A TOUR OF
Missouri Wineries

JONATHAN ECCHER
JEREMY HOLLINGSHEAD

Estate
PUBLISHERS LIMITED™

Estate Publishers Limited
106 Port Way
Columbia, Missouri 65201

Copyright © 2008 Estate Publishers Limited

All rights reserved

ISBN-13: 978-0-9817134-0-3
ISBN-10: 0-9817134-0-8

Authors: Jonathan Eccher and Jeremy Hollingshead
Production Directors: Jonathan Eccher and Jeremy Hollingshead
Designer: Clinton Johnson
Editor: Abby Callard
Contributing Writers: Abby Callard, Noelle Daly, Katherine Harmon, Rachel Kenny, Jennifer Meyer, and Joanna Schneider
Special Thanks: Missouri Wine & Grape Board
Cover Photo: Stone Hill Winery vineyard

Printed in China

Contact Estate Publishers Limited by:
E-mail at info@estatepublishers.com
Mail at 106 Port Way, Columbia, MO 65201
Phone at (314) 566-5671
Visiting www.estatepublishers.com

*To our families and friends,
which now includes each of Missouri's fine wineries ...*

Thank you.

Table of Contents

From grapevine... 1
The History of the Missouri Wine Industry 3
The Winemaking Process 6
Missouri Grape Varietals 10
Missouri Wine Regions 13
Augusta Region 15
    Augusta Winery 17
    Balducci Vineyards 19
    Montelle Winery 21
    Mount Pleasant Winery 25
    Sugar Creek Winery & Vineyards 29
    Yellow Farmhouse Vineyard & Winery 31
Central Region 33
    Baltimore Bend Vineyard 35
    Cooper's Oak Winery 37
    Crown Valley Port House 39
    Eichenberg Winery 41
    Grey Bear Vineyards & Winery 43
    Indian Creek Winery 45
    Les Bourgeois Vineyards & Winery 47
    Little Hills Winery & Restaurant 51
    Native Stone Winery 53
    Phoenix Winery & Vineyards 55
    Stone Hill Winery 57
    Summit Lake Winery 59
    The Eagle's Nest Winery 61
Hermann Region 63
    Adam Puchta & Son Winery 65
    Bias Vineyards & Winery 69
    Bommarito Estate Almond Tree Winery 71
    Hermannhof Winery & Vineyards 73
    OakGlenn Winery & Vineyard 77
    Röbller Vineyard Winery 79
    Stone Hill Winery 81
Ozark Highlands Region 85

Ferrigno Vineyards & Winery 87
Meramec Vineyards 89
Peaceful Bend Vineyard 91
Saint James Winery 93

Ozark Mountain Region 97
Le Cave Vineyards 99
Oovvda Winery 101
Stone Hill Winery 103
Wenwood Farm Winery 107
Westphalia Vineyards 109
Whispering Oaks Vineyard & Winery 111
White Rose Winery 113

Southeast Region 115
Cave Vineyard 117
Charleville Vineyards 119
Chaumette Vineyards & Winery 121
Claverach Farm & Vineyards 123
Crown Valley Champagne House 125
Crown Valley Winery 127
Durso Hills Vineyard & Winery 131
Hemman Winery 133
River Ridge Winery 135
Saint Francois Vineyard & Winery 137
Sainte Genevieve Winery 139
Tower Rock Winery 141
Twin Oaks Vineyard & Winery 143
Vance Vineyards & Winery 145
Villa Antonio Winery 147

West Region 149
Bynum Winery 151
Inland Sea Wines 153
Jowler Creek Winery 155
Montserrat Vineyards 157
New Oak Vineyards 159
Odessa Country Winery 161
Pirtle Winery 163
Riverwood Winery 165
Stonehaus Farms Vineyard & Winery 167
Terre Beau Vineyards & Winery 169

...to wineglass. 171

From grapevine …

The History of the Missouri Wine Industry

Missouri's wine industry has a very long and extremely rich history. From the first European immigrants settling the land and planting vineyards, through Missouri's dominance as the largest wine-producing state in the country and producer of the "Best Red Wine of All Nations," to its current state as a rapidly growing industry, reestablishing itself as one of the most unique and highest-quality wine-producing areas in both the country and the world.

The roots of the Missouri wine industry were planted in the early 1880s, when European immigrants began to settle throughout Missouri. The Augusta and Hermann regions saw the greatest influx of German immigrants, while the Ozark Highlands region became home to many Italian immigrants. These immigrants brought with them to Missouri the many rich traditions of their homeland. Among these was a love for winemaking.

For many years prior to the arrival of European immigrants, Native Americans had cultivated local grape varietals in Missouri. Although these varietals were new to the immigrants, because the climate and soil in Missouri were not conducive to growing the European varietals with which they were more familiar, they had no choice but to cultivate and develop these new varietals for their wines. As they came to find though, Missouri's native grape varietals produced very unique yet high-quality wines.

From that point, winemaking quickly grew throughout the state. In 1848, Missouri's winemakers produced less than 5,000 cases, but by 1856, production had grown to more than 40,000 cases per year. The Missouri wine industry continued to grow into the latter half of the 19th century, and by the 1880s, the state produced more than 800,000 cases annually, leading the nation, including California, in wine production.

At that time, Missouri wines were just as well known for their quality as they were for their quantity. At the 1873 Vienna World Exposition, a Norton wine produced in the Hermann region was declared the "Best Red Wine of All Nations." Henry Vizetelly, a noted wine critic of the day, predicted that Missouri Nortons would one day rival the great wines of Europe in both quality and quantity.

Worse for the European wine industry than the competition from Missouri's wines, a root louse began quickly destroying French vineyards in 1876, severely threatening France's wine industry. By 1880, nearly all French vineyards had been destroyed or severely damaged. As the epidemic threatened to cross French borders into neighboring countries, the Missouri wine industry came to the rescue. State entomologist Charles Riley discovered that some Missouri grape varietals were resistant to the louse and encouraged the sending of native-Missouri rootstocks to France. Hermann Jaeger, a Missouri winemaker, and George Hussman, a University of Missouri professor, grafted French vines onto healthy,

louse-resistant Missouri vines and shipped an estimated 10,000,000 rootstocks to France between 1885 and 1890 to be replanted in the French vineyards.

The same root louse that ravaged French vineyards soon also attacked vineyards in California. The California wine industry required importation of the Missouri-born, louse-resistant rootstocks from France to avoid the same fate that the French wine industry had faced. As a result, Missouri has its place in history as the savior of both the French and California wine industries.

Prior to 1920, more than 100 wineries existed in Missouri. Prohibition put a temporary end to the wine industry though, with the exception of Saint Stanislaus Seminary in Florissant, which continued to produce a small amount of sacramental wines. Vineyards were removed, used for other purposes, or just left untended, and winemaking facilities were either converted to serve other purposes or left to deteriorate. Prohibition ended in 1933, and although some wineries began producing wine again immediately after its end, serious production did not begin until the 1960s.

The Missouri wine industry's recovery really started in 1965, with the reopening of Stone Hill Winery in Hermann, followed by Mount Pleasant Winery in Augusta. As winemaking in Missouri continued to grow, the state began to regain recognition among wine lovers. The Augusta region became the first American Viticultural Area in 1980, followed by the Hermann region in 1983, the Ozark Mountain region in 1986, and the Ozark Highlands region in 1987.

Although Missouri's wine industry has yet to recover from Prohibition to the same degree that California's has, it is still flourishing. As Missourians, as well as wine lovers across the country and throughout the world, continue to discover the fine and unique award-winning wines that Missouri wineries have to offer, it is clear that Missouri's wine industry will only continue toward its pre-Prohibition glory.

The Winemaking Process

From grapevine to wine bottle, the process of winemaking is truly a science, an art even. Not only must the grapes be picked in the vineyard at just the right time, but they must be crushed and pressed at just the right pressure, the juices fermented with just the right amount of yeast and at just the right temperature, and the wines aged for just the right period of time. It is only through careful attention to detail throughout every step of the winemaking process that Missouri's winemakers are able to create such wonderful wines.

Harvesting:

The winemaking process begins, of course, with the picking, or harvesting, of grapes in the vineyard. Perfect timing in this first step is essential. The grapes must not only be picked at the proper point of ripeness, the exact time of which differs from year to year based on such factors as grape varietal, temperatures, amount of rainfall, and days of sunlight, but even at the right time of day. In Missouri, the harvest typically takes place from mid August through mid October, depending on the varietal. The result of this perfect timing by experienced harvesters is that the sugar content and acidity of the grapes are well balanced for the production of high-quality wines.

The grapes are harvested either by hand or by a machine grape harvester. Today, many wineries opt for the machine harvester, which is more efficient and can be operated at any time. For example, using a machine harvester, the grapes can be harvested very rapidly after bad weather hits, before they have a chance to rot, or even at night, when temperatures are lowest and the level of bitter phenolic compounds in the grapes is minimized. Still, other wineries prefer to harvest the grapes in the same way that their predecessors have for centuries: by hand, paying close attention to each grape.

Crushing and Pressing:

Once harvested, the grapes are quickly transported to the winery, where they are destemmed and crushed. The destemming and crushing machine first removes the grapes from their stems and then applies just enough pressure to break the grapes' skins so that their juices can be extracted. From the destemmer and crusher, the juices, skins, seeds, and pulps from the grapes, collectively known as the must, is pumped through a must chiller, which lowers its temperature. The must to be used in producing red wines then goes from the must chiller directly to the fermentation tanks, skins and all. The must for white and blush wines, on the other hand, goes from the must chiller to the grape press prior to reaching the fermentation tanks.

After crushing, the must for white and blush wines is pressed. The grape press is a large, cylindrical container with a rubber membrane affixed to its interior walls and a series of circular, perforated drainage channels periodically bisecting the container. Once the press is filled with the mixture of grape juices, skins, seeds, and pulps, the rubber membrane is gently inflated with air to slowly press the juices through the drainage channels to a collection basin outside the press. The juices are pressed slowly to minimize the bitter phenolic compounds from the skins released with the juices. After the pressure is maintained for a few minutes, the membrane deflates, and the press rotates to redistribute the must before repeating the cycle.

Fermentation:

After the pressing, the juices for white and blush wines meet back up with the must for the red wines in the fermentation area. After proper amounts of yeast are added, the white and blush wine juices are fermented in tanks at 50 to 65 degrees Fahrenheit, turning them from mere juices into wine. As the yeast and other solids begin to settle to the bottom of the tanks, the wine is pumped through a centrifuge, which separates them from the wine, preparing the wine for aging. For sweeter wines, the centrifuging is done earlier so that more of the grapes' natural sugars remain, as the longer the yeast remains, the more of the sugars are turned into alcohol.

The must used to produce red wines is fermented at a slightly-warmer 65 to 75 degrees Fahrenheit, and is done so prior to pressing. While fermenting, the juices are regularly stirred to aid in the extraction of pigments and tannins from the grape skins, which gives red wine its color. When the fermentation is complete, the wine is drained from the tanks and stored while the remaining solids are sent to the grape press for extraction of the last bit of wine.

Clarification:

Once fermentation is complete, the winemaker may choose to clarify the wine. In this optional step, winemakers rack or siphon the wine from one tank to another in an effort to leave the precipitates and solids, known as pomace, in the bottom of the tank. Some winemakers prefer to skip the clarification, allowing the pomace to remain in the wine for increased natural flavor. Filtering and fining also occur during this stage, further removing pomace from the wine. Through filtration, the wine passes through a filter that catches pomace. Fining is the addition of substances, such as egg whites, clay, or other compounds, to the wine that adhere to unwanted solids and force them to the bottom of the tank. After clarification, if this step is used, the wine is ready for aging or bottling.

Aging and Bottling:

The final step in the winemaking process is the aging and bottling of the wine. After fermentation and, if used by the winemaker, clarification, the wine is either bottled immediately or aged for some time. This aging typically takes place in a barrel made from either stainless steel or wood, with oak adding the most distinct flavor to the wine. Once the winemaker determines that the wine has reached a desired flavor, it is bottled and made ready for sale.

Throughout this amazing yet tedious winemaking process, Missouri's winemakers keep one goal in mind: to make the highest-quality wines possible to delight the taste buds of each Missouri wine lover. Winemaking is a science and an art, and nowhere is this more exemplified than in Missouri's rich wine industry.

Missouri Grape Varietals

Much of the world is familiar with such well-known and popular grape varietals as the Chardonnay, Merlot, and Zinfandel. While Missouri's climate and soil make it extremely difficult, if not impossible, to grow many such popular grapes, Missouri's wineries have found the climate and soil conducive to growing many other unique varietals, though no less delicious once made into wines. These varietals are the products of nearly two centuries of cultivation, experimentation, and hard work. In Missouri's unique grape varietals and wines, wine lovers have discovered some true hidden gems just waiting to explode onto the world wine scene.

CAYUGA   **CHAMBOURCIN**   **CHARDONEL**

Catawba:
The Catawba is typically used in the production of medium-bodied, sweet, fragrant, strawberry-like wines, which are traditionally served in casual, social settings.

Cayuga:
The Cayuga is a hybrid used to create light, fragrant, fruity, semi-dry white wines. Cayuga wines are enjoyable alone or with light foods and appetizers.

Chambourcin:
The Chambourcin produces medium-bodied red wines similar to a Pinot Noir. With a fruity aroma and cherry, earthy, and spicy complexities, its wines are best served with barbecue, pork, or pasta dishes.

Chancellor or Chancellor Noir:
The Chancellor, also called the Chancellor Noir, is a hybrid that makes fresh, young wines, with berry flavors and herbal scents.

Chardonel:
The Chardonel is a cross between the popular Chardonnay and the Seyval. Its wines are usually barrel fermented, very dry, and full bodied, and great with heavy seafood dishes, chicken, and cream sauces.

Concord:
Used to produce "America's original dessert wine," the Concord is famous for its deep purple color and classic sweetness. The intense fruity flavors brought out in its wines make them perfect for after-dinner sipping.

Norton or Cynthiana:
The official grape of the State of Missouri, the Norton, also called the Cynthiana, produces rich, full-bodied, dry red wines that can be similar in style to a Cabernet Sauvignon. Its wines have the spicy overtones of a Zinfandel complemented by nice berry flavors, creating wines that go well with red meats, smoked meats, and wild game.

NORTON **VIDAL** **VIGNOLES**

Saint Vincent:

The Saint Vincent is a hybrid that makes elegant red wines and is perfect for Nouveau-style wines in the fall. Its wines may also take on Burgundy-like characteristics, or occasionally be unusually sweet. Saint Vincent wines are great when served slightly chilled with pork, veal, and barbecue.

Seyval:

The Seyval makes clean, crisp, medium-bodied white wines. With fresh herbal flavors, its wines are similar in style to a Chenin Blanc. Barrel-fermented Seyval wines takes on an oak complexity indicative of a Chardonnay, and they pair well with pork, Asian dishes, and rich cream-based and butter-based sauces.

Traminette:

The Traminette is a late- to mid-season grape that produces wines similar to a Gewurztraminer. The elegant floral aroma and wonderful spicy flavor of its wines provide nice complements to Asian, poultry, and seafood dishes.

Vidal:

The Vidal is used to make dry to semi-dry, full-bodied white wines with fruity characteristics, somewhat like dry Italian wines. The clean, citrus flavors of lemon and grapefruit found in Vidal wines are great matches for seafoods and poultry.

Vignoles:

The Vignoles is one of Missouri's most-versatile grapes. It is used to produce wines ranging from dry white wines to sweet, late-harvest dessert wines. The luscious floral aroma and fruity flavors of pineapple and apricot found in Vignoles wines are reminiscent of a German Riesling. The wines are ideal to be served with Chinese food, fresh fruit, and fruit desserts.

Missouri Wine Regions

AUGUSTA

Augusta Winery
Balducci Vineyards
Montelle Winery
Mount Pleasant Winery
Sugar Creek Winery & Vineyards
Yellow Farmhouse Vineyard & Winery

CENTRAL

Baltimore Bend Vineyard
Cooper's Oak Winery
Crown Valley Port House
Eichenberg Winery
Grey Bear Vineyards & Winery
Indian Creek Winery
Les Bourgeois Vineyards & Winery
Little Hills Winery & Restaurant
Native Stone Winery
Phoenix Winery & Vineyards
Stone Hill Winery
Summit Lake Winery
The Eagle's Nest Winery

HERMANN

Adam Puchta & Son Winery
Bias Vineyards & Winery
Bommarito Estate Almond Tree Winery
Hermannhof Winery & Vineyards
OakGlenn Winery & Vineyard
Röbller Vineyard Winery
Stone Hill Winery

OZARK HIGHLANDS

Ferrigno Vineyards & Winery
Meramec Vineyards
Peaceful Bend Vineyard
Saint James Winery

OZARK MOUNTAIN

Le Cave Vineyards
Oovvda Winery
Stone Hill Winery
Wenwood Farm Winery
Westphalia Vineyards
Whispering Oaks Vineyard & Winery
White Rose Winery

SOUTHEAST

Cave Vineyard
Charleville Vineyards
Chaumette Vineyards & Winery
Claverach Farm & Vineyards
Crown Valley Champagne House
Crown Valley Winery
Durso Hills Vineyard & Winery
Hemman Winery
River Ridge Winery
Saint Francois Vineyard & Winery
Sainte Genevieve Winery
Tower Rock Winery
Twin Oaks Vineyard & Winery
Vance Vineyards & Winery
Villa Antonio Winery

WEST

Bynum Winery
Inland Sea Wines
Jowler Creek Winery
Montserrat Vineyards
New Oak Vineyards
Odessa Country Winery
Pirtle Winery
Riverwood Winery
Stonehaus Farms Vineyard & Winery
Terre Beau Vineyards & Winery

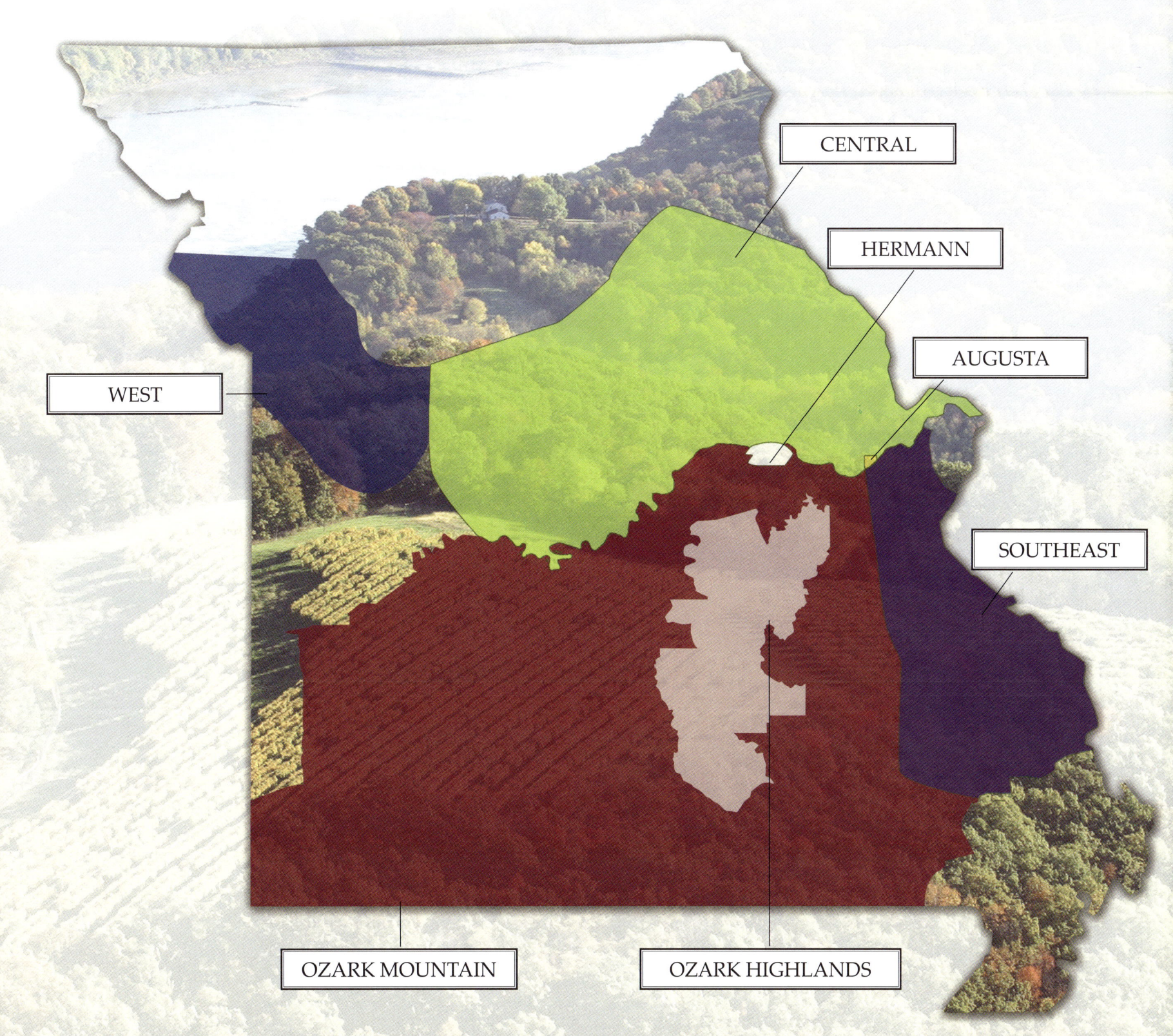

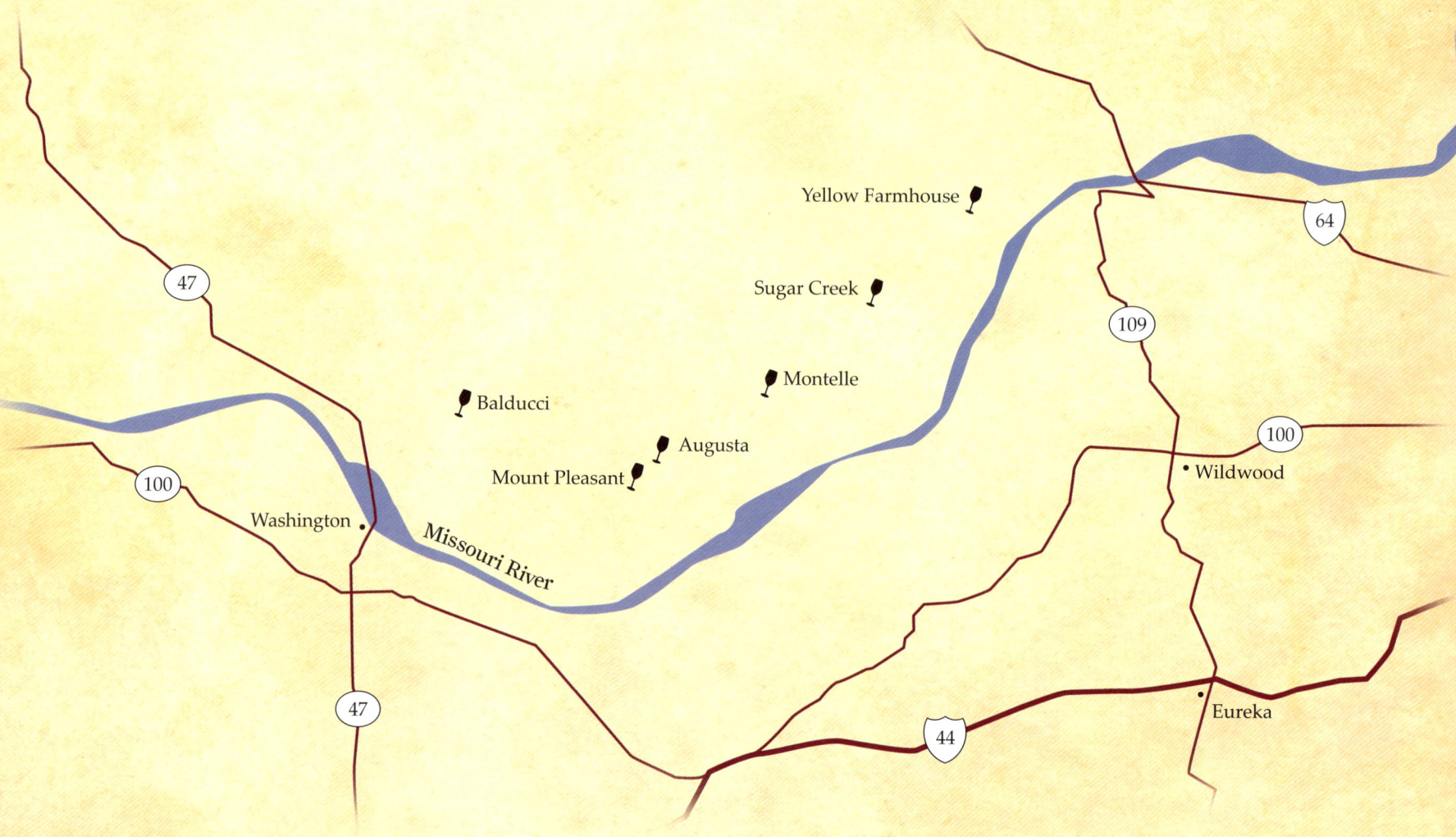

Although small, encompassing only 15 square miles, the Augusta region has already found its place in American Viticultural Area history: The region was the first official American Viticultural Area in the country, gaining the status on June 20, 1980. Not until eight months later did the Napa Valley American Viticultural Area in northern California even reach the same status.

The region is centered around the town of Augusta, just a short drive from the busy metropolis of Saint Louis, where German immigrants first settled in the early 1800s after being reminded of their homeland. Immediately after arriving, they continued their proud tradition of winemaking that they brought with them from Germany. By 1850, the region was already a firmly-established wine region, and among the top-producing regions in Missouri, which produced more wine than even California at that time. Although Prohibition halted the wine industry temporarily, the region's wineries have since reestablished it as one of Missouri's, as well as America's, finest wine-producing regions.

Today, the stretch of State Highway 94 between Defiance and Marthasville has so many wineries along it that the highway has been nicknamed the Missouri Weinstrasse, German for "Wine Road." A drive down it takes visitors from winery to winery and offers scenic views of the hills, valleys, and quaint villages passing by. Still, a stop in the town of Augusta is always worthwhile, whether to taste the wines of the Augusta region or to enjoy the charm and ambiance of a town where times seems to stand still.

Augusta Winery

Owners: Tony & Cindy Kooyumjian
Winemaker: Tony Kooyumjian
Region: Augusta

Established: 1988
Vineyard Acreage: 45 acres
Annual Production: 15,000 cases

Perched upon a spectacular bluff overlooking the Missouri River Valley, Augusta Winery has it all: a beautiful location, rich history, numerous awards, and even more importantly for a winery, many acres of land ideal for growing the highest quality of grapes.

Since the founding of the town of Augusta in 1836, vineyards have existed because of the area's unique soil and excellent grape-growing climate. In 1998, over a century and a half later, owner and winemaker Tony Kooyumjian realized Mother Nature's gift to the area and set himself a lofty goal: to establish a vineyard and produce the highest-quality wines in the region. At that moment, Augusta Winery was born.

The winery has seen great success as a result of Kooyumjian's meticulous planning and hard work. Its wines, which are made from grapes harvested in its own beautiful, 45-acre vineyard, have won numerous awards throughout the country, including the 2004, 2006, and 2007 Governor's Cups for the single best wine in Missouri. While Augusta's 2003 Chambourcin and 2004 Norton have received more recognition than others, the winery clearly produces countless other award-winning wines, such as its 2004 Norton Reserva del Patrón and 2006 Icewine, each of which has received a gold medal at the Missouri Wine Competition. Augusta produces only in small quantities to guarantee that this same, unmatched quality is consistent across its wines.

To accommodate the many visitors who cannot get enough of its fine wines, the winery is open year round and allows them to sample its many excellent wines free of charge in its tasting room. The wide selection of wines on Augusta's wine list ranges from dry dinner wines to sweet dessert wines, and ensures that any visitor can find that perfect wine. On warm days, visitors can even enjoy a lovely bottle of Augusta wine outside on a covered terrace overlooking the beautiful countryside. Soda, water, and locally-produced cheeses and sausages are also available to complement Augusta's wines and to keep even the youngest visitors happy. Before heading home, visitors may browse the gift shop, where Augusta wines, gift baskets, gift certificates, and other wine-related merchandise are available. Even more fun, Augusta allows visitors to order custom-labeled bottles of its wines, printed with any unique wording desired.

Those looking for a special treat travel to the town of Augusta in early December each year to enjoy the its annual Candlelight Christmas Walk. Luminaries line the streets of the community, lighting the way to shops, restaurants, and of course, Augusta Winery, where visitors are able to get out of the cold and warm themselves with a glass of the winery's Vintage Port.

With stunning views, a storied history, and spectacular wines, Augusta Winery offers something for everyone.

Augusta Winery

5601 High Street
Augusta, Missouri 63332
(636) 228-4301
www.augustawinery.com

BELOW: *Augusta is open year round and offers visitors free tastings of its amazing wines.*

A man will be eloquent if you give him good wine.

— Ralph Waldo Emerson

Balducci Vineyards

Owners: Rick & Carol Balducci

Region: Augusta

Established: 2001

Vineyard Acreage: 8 acres

Annual Production: 2,500 cases

In 1906, Pat and Angela Balducci emigrated from Italy to the United States in search of a new life. They brought with them a Tuscan tradition of love for fine wines and foods, and they put their talents to good use in the restaurant and grocery industries. Pat and Angela worked hard to build a happy life, gave birth to a baby boy in 1915, and gained great respect in the community.

Years later, their grown son, Louis, took a job working in a California vineyard, an experience that sparked his interest in the wine industry. After returning to Saint Louis in 1946 following a stint in World War II, Louis opened the Balducci Wine Distributing Company. He became a highly-respected wine specialist in Missouri, and his reputation as a speaker and wine educator grew throughout the entire Midwest.

In 1988, owners Rick and Carol Balducci rekindled their Italian relative's legacy in the Missouri wine industry by naming their winery operation Louis P. Balducci Vineyards, though they have since shortened it to Balducci Vineyards. The winery is perched atop a hill overlooking 76 acres of rolling hills, farmland, and vineyards, and sits next to a restored 1860s farmhouse and two antique barns. The Balducci family's Tuscan heritage is evident in the winery's beautiful tasting room, which is surrounded by a covered veranda and scenic terraces.

Balducci's wines are as impressive as its winery. Eight premium wines, ranging from dry to sweet, are available to tantalize the taste buds of any visitor. Cheeses, sausages, and freshly-baked breads are available to complement the fine Aria, Chiaretto, Dolce Bianco, Natalia, Norton, Port, Sonata, and Vidal Blanc wines.

Balducci also offers a delicious Italian menu to match the quality of its wines. With 33 years of experience at the famous Balducci's Winefest Restaurant in Saint Louis, the

Balduccis are able to offer visitors top-notch Italian food in a rustic yet elegant setting. Menu items include baked brie; an Italian salad prepared with romaine and iceberg lettuce, mushrooms, artichoke hearts, olives, red onions, and Italian cheeses; and Chicken Vignoles, a breaded-and-baked chicken breast topped with a lemon-mushroom wine sauce and served with linguini. Other traditional Italian offerings, such as cannelloni, seafood pasta, and the winery's award-winning pizzas and toasted ravioli, are also available. Balducci offers visitors inside seating, with tables available next to the gas-burning stove, as well as outdoor seating in the enclosed, heated porch that features multiple fireplaces. To visitors' delight, Balducci also provides live musical entertainment on its spacious, outdoor terrace on weekends from April through October.

Balducci has gained both local and national notoriety. The breathtaking winery was chosen as the backdrop for a national Amtrak advertising campaign, which was featured in such prominent publications as *Time, Newsweek,* and *Better Homes and Gardens*, and the area is listed in *Reader's Digest* as one the most scenic drives in America. Additionally, Balducci has been voted "Favorite Winery" in *Concierge Magazine*'s readers' poll and receives the same recognition year after year in the *Washington Missourian*. Clearly, Balducci is one of Missouri's hidden gems and should not be missed by any wine lover.

Balducci Vineyards

6601 Highway 94 South
Augusta, Missouri 63332
(636) 482-8466
www.balduccivineyards.com

ABOVE: Visitors are welcome to try any of Balducci's eight wonderful wines in its beautiful tasting room.

RIGHT: The restored 1860s farmhouse and two antique barns help make Balducci the perfect combination of past and present.

Within the bottle's depths, the wine's soul sang one night.

— Charles Baudelaire

Montelle Winery

Owners: Tony & Cindy Kooyumjian
Winemaker: Tony Kooyumjian
Region: Augusta

Established: 1970
Vineyard Acreage: 69 acres
Annual Production: 17,800 cases

History lives in the magnificent wines produced by Montelle Winery. Located in the Augusta region, Montelle preserves a tradition of excellence that began centuries ago. Prior to Prohibition, the region played a major role in making Missouri the largest wine-producing state in the entire United States, and Montelle is doing its part today to restore the state and the region to their previous glory.

As visitors travel southward across the Missouri River into Saint Charles County and turn onto Highway 94, they begin to take a step back in time, entering an area well known for its Lewis and Clark Trail, Daniel Boone Settlement, and Missouri's Weinstrasse, German for "Wine Road." Many Germans immigrated to the Augusta region in the early 1800s and built beautiful communities there, where they found the rich soil to be perfect for grape growing. Winemaking in the region flourished throughout the 19th century and into the 20th, until Prohibition brought it to a halt.

In the late 1960s and early 1970s though, a few pioneering souls began to revive the old vineyards and winery buildings. One of these pioneers, Clayton Byers, founded the winery in 1970 that would soon become Montelle. After merging with another winery fourteen years later, the winery was finally purchased by current

owners Tony and Cindy Kooyumjian in 1998. Montelle sits among the beautiful vineyards just outside the historic town of Augusta. The town, which lies just 35 miles from Saint Louis and is a perfect day or weekend retreat, maintains an Old-World charm in its many original buildings housing craft shops, antique emporiums, taverns, and restaurants.

Montelle is located on a 20-acre property high atop Osage Ridge, 400 feet above the Missouri River, and its outdoor terrace offers visitors glorious views of the river valley, town of Augusta, and nearby farms and wineries below. At sunset, the views are unmatched. Although the spectacular views make a visit to Montelle special in their own right, it is the winery's impressive wine list that keeps visitors returning time and time again. Montelle wines are extremely accomplished, with 18 of them winning awards in 2007 alone in such prestigious competitions as the Missouri Wine Competition and the Pacific Rim International.

Montelle's wine list is both extensive and delicious, ranging from such smooth whites as the Seyval and Vignoles to the distinguished reds of Chambourcin and Cynthiana. The winery has gone to extra lengths to perfect its German-style white wines as a tribute to Augusta's rich German history. Montelle is also noted for its delicious fruit and dessert wines, which include the semi-sweet Strawberry, the sweet-but-not-too-sweet Blackberry, and the robust Raspberry Port.

Montelle Winery

201 Montelle Drive
Augusta, Missouri 63332
(888) 595-9463
www.montelle.com

BELOW: Montelle Winery's outdoor terrace provides a wonderful place for visitors to enjoy wines in fine weather.

Still, it is the winery's Saint Wenceslaus that many visitors find most intriguing, especially during the holidays. This red wine, infused with a special mixture of herbs and spices, is released at Thanksgiving each year and offered during the cold winter months. With such a great selection of fine wines, Montelle is sure to have a wine or two to delight any visitor's taste.

While its wines are more than enough to entice any visitor, Montelle offers much more. The recently-opened Klondike Café serves Starbucks coffees, lattes, chai teas, and iced drinks, and provides wireless internet service reaching all the way to the outdoor terrace. The Café also serves a large menu featuring freshly-baked breads, gourmet sandwiches, and pizzas, and even creates custom party platters to feed groups as large as 10.

Montelle's visitors can also enjoy a number of other special treats. During warm months,

ABOVE: The view from the winery itself is worth the trip.

BELOW: Visitors love stepping up to Montelle's elegant tasting counter.

the winery's well-known sunset dinners delight visitors with a delicious three-course meal topped off by a special chef's-choice dessert, and fun, live music is played on the winery's terrace on most weekends from April through mid November. During colder months, Montelle is still a wonderful stop for visitors enjoying the Christmas-time charm of Augusta. In fact, the winery's Raspberry Port and Saint Wenceslaus have become favorites among those in Augusta for the town's annual Christmas Candlelight Walk.

Montelle fascinates wine lovers from near and far, and the drive to the winery only adds to the experience. The winding country road that leads to Montelle offers unforgettable views of rolling hills, lovely meadows, rich farmland, and towering bluffs. Still, the landscape only prefaces the beauty that awaits visitors at Montelle.

ABOVE: *Montelle entertains visitors of all ages.*

RIGHT: *The winery is a popular destination for those seeking great wines and fun times.*

"
It's true, some wines improve with age. But only if the grapes were good in the first place.

— Abigail Van Buren

Mount Pleasant Winery

Owner: Charles Dressel
Winemaker: Mark Baehmann
Region: Augusta

Established: 1859
Vineyard Acreage: 85 acres
Annual Production: 46,000 cases

When brothers Friedrich Münch and Georg Münch saw the beautiful hilltops and majestic Missouri River Valley after immigrating to the United States and arriving in the Augusta region, they were reminded of their home in Germany. It was on this land that the Munch brothers founded Mount Pleasant Winery in 1859, a century and a half ago. Today, the winery's award-winning wines are still aged in the original hand-dug cellars, bringing together Mount Pleasant's rich history and modern-day success in making award-winning wines.

Due to the great time and effort that went into the main building, made from limestone and wood found in the area, and the hand-dug cellars, construction of the winery was not completed until 1881. After its complete construction, Mount Pleasant continued to flourish for nearly half a century longer before Prohibition forced the winery to rip its grapevines from the ground and shut down its winemaking operation. Fortunately for Missouri wine lovers, in 1966, vines were replanted, and Mount Pleasant reopened its winemaking operation and doors to the public.

Today, the winery, which is located only a short distance from Saint Louis, offers a wonderful escape from the city.

ABOVE: Mount Pleasant is quite popular among Missouri's wine lovers.

— 25 —

Impressively, it is the largest winery in Missouri practicing sustainable viticulture, an integrated system of growing grapes in an economically-viable, socially-supportive, and ecologically-sound way. Mount Pleasant's geographic location, with bluffs providing a natural barrier from frosts and floods and hillsides offering ideal sunlight and drainage, also lends itself to the growing of high-quality grapes.

Among its 85 acres of vineyards, Mount Pleasant grows Cabernet Sauvignon, Chambourcin, Chardonnay, Merlot, Norton, Rayon d'Or, Saint Vincent, Vidal Blanc, and Vignoles grapevines, and is always looking to introduce new varietals. One of its recent introductions was of Pinot Noir vines. While the Pinot Noir varietal is not native to Missouri and will be very difficult, if not impossible, to grow in this climate, if successful, Mount Pleasant will be the first winery in Missouri to produce its own Pinot Noir grapes.

A rarity in the Missouri wine industry, many of Mount Pleasant's wines meet the requirements to be labeled as "Estate Bottled," which designates their combined growing and production conditions. The requirements for the

Mount Pleasant Winery

5634 High Street
Augusta, Missouri 63332
(636) 482-9463
www.mountpleasant.com

ABOVE: Weddings do not get much more beautiful than at Mount Pleasant.

RIGHT: High-quality grapes make for the winery's high-quality wines.

"Estate Bottled" label are very strict and require, among other things, that Mount Pleasant and the vineyards where all of the grapes are grown are located in the same viticultural area, that the winery owns or controls the vineyards where the grapes are grown, and that its wines are produced in one continuous process, without ever leaving Mount Pleasant's property. By producing "estate bottled" wines, Mount Pleasant ensures that visitors receive only the most-exclusive locally-made wines possible.

Not only are many of its wines "estate bottled," but all of them are of the highest quality. The winery's 2005 Claret was awarded a double gold medal at the Tasters Guild International Wine Competition, and its 2004 Norton received a gold medal in both the Tasters Guild International and the Los Angeles International Wine & Spirits Competitions. Its quality not just limited to a couple fine wines, 10 Mount Pleasant wines took home medals at the 2007 Missouri Wine Competition. Additionally, its wines have been served across the globe, the winery was voted "Favorite Winery" in Sauce Magazine's 2007 Readers' Poll, and even Tipper Gore herself, wife of former Vice President Al Gore, has mentioned a Mount Pleasant wine as one of her personal favorites.

To enjoy its wines, Mount Pleasant welcomes visitors to its spacious 4,000-square-foot tasting room. In pleasant weather, the winery's terrace offers spectacular views of the Missouri River Valley in a comfortable setting. To complement the wines, visitors can purchase delicious picnic foods from Mount Pleasant's Grocery and Grill. Live

ABOVE: Mount Pleasant invites visitors to find out what a fine winery should be.

ABOVE: Even Mount Pleasant's gate is accented by pristine landscaping and careful attention to detail.

music, winery and cellar tours, winemaker's dinners, and holiday-themed events keep the winery busy and visitors smiling year round.

Visitors can now enjoy a taste of Mount Pleasant without traveling all the way to Augusta. In April 2008, the winery opened a second location in the popular tourist destination of Branson. Located on a two-acre piece of property on Green Mountain Drive, near world-famous 76 Country Music Boulevard, Mount Pleasant's Branson location offers visitors a fun place to unwind between visits to other attractions, or an entire day of fun and wine tasting. With 1,500 square feet of tasting rooms, a 3,000-square-foot retail area, and a specially-made 600-gallon French-oak barrel from which visitors can bottle their own wines, there is plenty for any visitor to enjoy.

As one of Missouri's oldest and finest wineries, Mount Pleasant offers a wonderful combination of rich history and modern quality that no wine lover should miss.

ABOVE: Mount Pleasant's cellar allows visitors to take a step back in time.

BELOW: Each of Mount Pleasant's wines starts in the vineyard.

The peoples of the Mediterranean began to emerge from barbarism when they learnt to cultivate the olive and the vine.

— Thucydides

Sugar Creek Winery & Vineyards

Owners: Ken & Becky Miller
Winemaker: Chris Lorch
Region: Augusta

Established: 1994
Vineyard Acreage: 11 acres
Annual Production: 5,500 cases

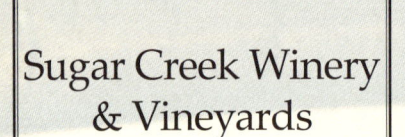

Sugar Creek Winery & Vineyards

125 Boone Country Lane
Defiance, Missouri 63341
(636) 987-2400
www.sugarcreekwines.com

Located on both the Katy Trail and Augusta's Missouri Weinstrasse, Sugar Creek Winery & Vineyards is a family-owned winery that provides a gathering place for Katy Trail travelers and wine enthusiasts alike. While the winery offers breathtaking views and a relaxing atmosphere to delight any visitor, Sugar Creek is a popular wine lover's destination for another reason: Sugar Creek's 2006 Cynthiana won "Best of Show" at the inaugural National Norton Wine Competition, as the best overall Norton wine out of more than 150 entered from across the United States.

Years ago, owning a winery was just a dream for owners Ken and Becky Miller. While having a meal at a Bob Evans restaurant one day though, tears filled Becky's eyes as they made the decision to actually turn their dream into a reality. In August 1994, the Millers took the first step in creating Sugar Creek by purchasing Boone Country Winery, a small country winery producing very little wine. Today, the Millers wake up each morning to the fruits of their labor: a very fine winery producing some of Missouri's highest-quality wines.

Wine experts agree that great wines get their start in the vineyard. Sugar Creek's location high on a bluff overlooking the Missouri River Valley and the vineyard's unique soil composition create conditions that are ideal for grape growing. Adding the finishing touch in the vineyard is the skilled work of the Millers' son, Chris Lorch, who spent two years working in the vineyard at Plump Jack Winery in California's Napa Valley. The natural result of these factors is the production of grapes of extraordinary quality for use in the wines made at Sugar Creek.

The winery grows Chambourcin, Chardonel,

Cynthiana, and Vidal grapes for use in its wide selection of unique and flavorful wines. Aside from being of such fine quality, Sugar Creek wines pair very well with a wide range of foods, and the Millers are always happy to help visitors select that perfect wine for any food. For instance, a fruity, medium-body red, the Chambourcin pairs well with barbecue, pork, and pasta dishes. The Cynthiana is a big, bold red that really brings out the flavor of any red meat. The Chardonel complements heavy seafood dishes and cream-based sauces very well. Finally, the Vidal is a crisp, citrussy wine that goes nicely with light seafood dishes and poultry.

Sugar Creek offers visitors a wonderful setting in which to enjoy its world-class wines. On weekends from April through October, visitors can take in live music in the gazebo as they enjoy delicious snacks and, of course, a bottle of Sugar Creek wine. When there is a chill in the air, visitors can take their wines inside to the cozy parlor and tasting room, located in the winery's turn-of-the-century Victorian home.

As wine lovers are coming to find, Sugar Creek is quietly making a lot of noise with the quality of its wines. If nothing else, its "Best of Show" Cynthiana should not be missed. As the judges at the inaugural National Norton Wine Competition declared, this wine is the finest that Missouri has to offer.

ABOVE: Sugar Creek welcomes all visitors with its warm, country hospitality.

RIGHT: The winery's covered, outdoor patio lets visitors enjoy a fine bottle of wine in rain or shine.

"*It is not a wine that commands your attention, but rather rewards it.*

— Dave Guimond

Yellow Farmhouse Vineyard & Winery

Yellow Farmhouse Vineyard & Winery

100 Defiance Road
Defiance, Missouri 63341
(314) 409-6139
www.yellowfarmhousewines.com

Owner: Dale Rollings
Winemaker: Dale Rollings
Region: Augusta

Established: 2004
Vineyard Acreage: 3 acres
Annual Production: 400 cases

Set in a deep valley west of Saint Louis, just back from the bank of the Missouri River, lies the tiny town of Defiance. With a population of only 50, Defiance does not change much, though it does remain popular among bicyclists and weekend motorcyclists. Highway 94 winds unassumingly through the town, past quaint houses with white picket fences, until it reaches the edge of town and leads visitors right up to Yellow Farmhouse Vineyard & Winery.

The winery's property has an interesting history. Originally, a blacksmith's shop stood on the property, and the general store that followed was a popular resting point for those traveling by horse to Saint Louis. Although no remnants of the blacksmith's shop exist, the foundation of the general store still lies just below the surface of Yellow Farmhouse's front lawn. In the 1920s, a bright-yellow house was built, and the barn that now houses the winemaking facility, was constructed shortly after the house.

The seeds of Yellow Farmhouse were planted in owner Dale Rollings' head as early as the 1990s, at which time Rollings was an avid basement winemaker. While

— 31 —

living and working near Saint Charles, he noticed that the grapes harvested in the area were increasing in quality with each passing year. Clearly, the land was ripe for grape growing.

In 2004, Rollings acquired a rundown bed and breakfast that would become Yellow Farmhouse. Knowing that grapevines grow best on hillsides, Rollings planted the winery's first vines in spring 2005 on a hillside overlooking the Missouri River Valley. With these Norton vines growing surpisingly well, Rollings immediately purchased another small piece of land just west of Yellow Farmhouse, and by April 2006, had planted Traminette vines to provide a nice complement to the Norton vines.

From its vineyards' grapes, Yellow Farmhouse produces a handful of very delightful wines, including a light, off-dry white made from Traminette grapes, which is similar to a German Gewurztraminer. In addition to its estate-grown Norton and Traminette, the winery also produces a Chambourcin, Chardonel, and Vignoles. As another unique offering, Yellow Farmhouse makes four different mustards, including a Curry Mustard, Garlic Aioli Mustard, Horseradish Mustard, and Stone-Ground Mustard.

The winery provides an incredibly-nice setting for a summer evening, where visitors love heading to Yellow Farmhouse's deck or to the hill above the winery with some wines, cheeses, and fruits, to just enjoy life. As its owner proudly explains, Yellow Farmhouse is not big, and that is exactly how it was intended to be.

RIGHT: Visitors can sample great wines at the winery's tasting room bar.

LEFT: Yellow Farmhouse's tasting room is a comfortable setting for visitors to sample wines.

" *Wine is inspiring and adds greatly to the joy of living.*

— Napoleon Bonaparte

Central Region

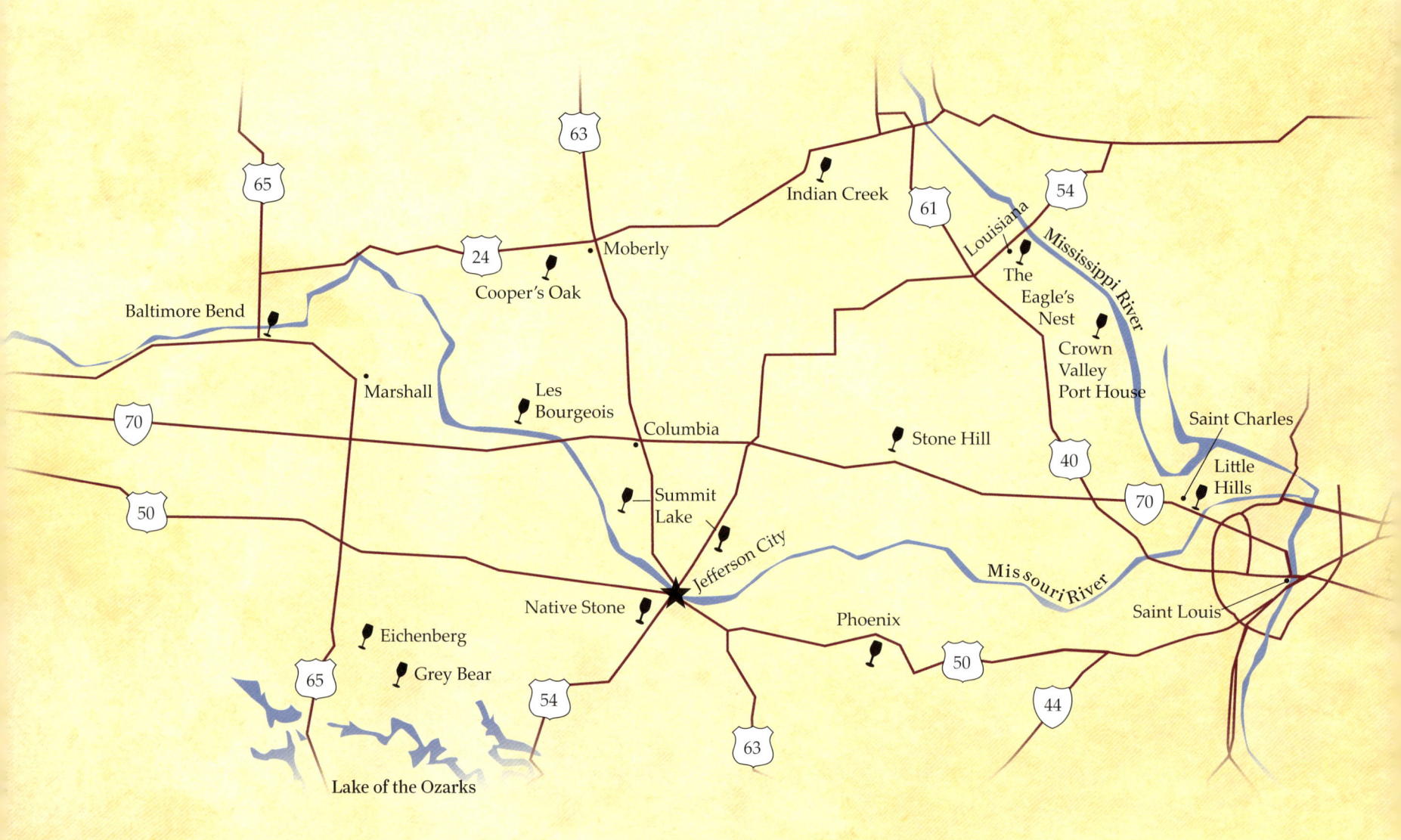

The Central region stretches from U.S. Highway 65 in western Missouri east to the Mississippi River and south as far as the Lake of the Ozarks. With such a large geographic area, the wineries of the region are spread across varying terrains, from towering cliffs to low-lying river valleys, and exposed to different climates and weather conditions. The result is a selection of wines with the greatest diversity of any of the seven regions.

The region also offers visitors as much diversity in its attractions and activities as across its wines. For visitors interested in Missouri's rich history, Jefferson City, Columbia, and Fulton are perfect destinations. In the state capital of Jefferson City, visitors can tour the Capitol building to catch a glimpse of where the state's legislative activity has taken place since 1917. Among other attractions, Columbia is home to the University of Missouri's flagship campus. The University was established in 1839 as the first public university west of the Mississippi River. Just north of Jefferson City and east of Columbia is Fulton, home of Westminster College, where Winston Churchill delivered his infamous "Iron Curtain" speech in 1946.

Whether discovering its rich history, or enjoying the many activities available, including those at the popular Lake of the Ozarks, visitors are sure to find plenty to do throughout the Central region.

Baltimore Bend Vineyard

Owners: Richard & Kathleen Livingston, Scott Livingston, & Sarah Schmidt

Winemaker: Richard Livingston

Region: Central

Established: 2003

Vineyard Acreage: 7 acres

Annual Production: 3,000 cases

The philosophy at Baltimore Bend is that the grapes make the wines. Fortunately for wine lovers, the land at Baltimore Bend has had ten thousand years to prepare itself to produce the highest-quality grapes. During the last Ice Age, the area around Baltimore Bend Vineyard marked the southern edge of the North American glacier fields. As the ice retreated, strong winds deposited fertile, silt-rich soil across the region that is now central Missouri, the same soil that still exists throughout the region today providing winemakers ideal soil for grape growing.

Nearly ten thousand years later, Baltimore Bend is taking advantage of this rich soil, producing award-winning wine after award-winning wine, all while having been opened for only a few short years. The vineyard itself was started in 1997, with just under two acres of grapevines planted, and the vineyard expanded three times, in 1999, 2001, and 2006. Today, Baltimore Bend's vineyard contains a total of seven acres of Cabernet Franc, Chambourcin, Chardonel, Cynthiana, and Vignoles grapevines.

From the grapes grown in its vineyard, Baltimore Bend produces several excellent, dry red wines. Its 2004 Cynthiana received a gold medal at the Mid-America Wine Competition, and its 2004 Chambourcin received a silver medal. Baltimore Bend's Chardonel is also a medal

ABOVE: Baltimore Bend's lush vineyard is the birthplace of excellent wine.

winner, as are several of its original blends and a number of its sweet fruit wines. While less recognized than its award-winning counterparts, the winery's Peach and Apple wines are just as unique and delicious. All Baltimore Bend wines are available for tasting and purchase in the winery's tasting room, as well as at a number of select locations throughout the state.

From the outside, Baltimore Bend looks like a rustic, 19th-century restaurant or saloon, but the modern equipment and sleek granite tasting counter located inside remind visitors that Baltimore Bend provides only the most contemporary accommodations. The winery prides itself on its casual approach to wine. It makes a point to emphasize that wine tasting at Baltimore Bend is not offered by pretentious wine gurus, but rather by down-to-earth, wine-loving Midwesterners. Periodically, educational classes are even offered on such topics as pairing wines with chocolates or cheeses. Whether as part of a class or while simply getting away from the stresses of life, visitors always find a full glass of Baltimore Bend wine to be a delightful complement to the winery's beautiful scenery.

Baltimore Bend Vineyard

27150 Highway 24
Waverly, Missouri 64096
(660) 493-0258
www.baltimorebend.com

ABOVE: *The tasting room's rustic exterior is a nice contrast to its modern interior.*

RIGHT: *Even owners Richard and Kathleen Livingston find time to enjoy a great glass of Baltimore Bend wine.*

"*I cook with wine. Sometimes I even add it to the food.*

— W.C. Fields

Cooper's Oak Winery

Owners: Matthew & Michelle Kirby
Winemaker: Matthew Kirby
Region: Central

Established: 2006
Vineyard Acreage: 4 acres
Annual Production: 1,000 cases

Cooper's Oak Winery

96-A West Jones Street
Higbee, Missouri 65257
(660) 456-7507
www.coopersoakwinery.com

Set amidst the hills of north-central Missouri, Cooper's Oak Winery offers visitors both a great selection of wines and an interesting, rarely-seen glimpse into the barrel-making process. Cooper's Oak is uniquely and conveniently located on the same grounds, as well as owned by members of the same family, as A & K Cooperage, a manufacturer of fine American-oak wine barrels.

ABOVE: A tour of the vineyard at Cooper's Oak is fun for friends and family alike.

Although Cooper's Oak did not open its doors until April 2007, owner Matthew Kirby is far from inexperienced in the wine industry. After finishing school, Matthew joined his father, Dale Kirby, and grandfather, D. L. Andrews, in the family business at A & K Cooperage, manufacturing barrels for use in winemaking. After getting a taste of the wine industry, Matthew's interest led him to begin experimenting with home winemaking kits. Taking advantage of his contacts made over the years in both the California and the Missouri wine industries, as well as his growing knowledge of winemaking, Matthew turned his dream into reality by establishing Cooper's Oak.

Cooper's Oak has quickly developed an extensive wine list, which features such Missouri wines as Chambourcin, Norton, Saint Vincent, and Vidal. The winery also uses grapes from California to be able to offer such popular wines as Cabernet Sauvignon, Merlot, and

Syrah. Additionally, Cooper's Oak produces two delightful table wines: Michelle's Sweet Red and Michelle's Sweet White, both named for owner Michelle Kirby.

While Cooper's Oak is located on the same grounds as A & K Cooperage, it also sits conveniently next to Carol's Barrels and Antiques, an antique shop owned by Matthew's mother. After selecting that perfect bottle of Cooper's Oak wine, visitors can choose from an assortment of sausages, cheeses, and crackers at Carol's and enjoy the wine and snacks on the antique shop's patio, where aromas from the barrel factory further delight the senses.

To share a unique look into the wine industry, Cooper's Oak is pleased to offer tours of both the winery and the barrel-making facility to groups of all sizes. From a great selection of wines to an all-inclusive look into a rarely-seen aspect of the winemaking industry, Cooper's Oak really does have it all.

ABOVE: *Cooper's Oak sits on the same grounds as A & K Cooperage, maker of world-class American-oak wine barrels.*

LEFT: *Owner and winemaker Matthew Kirby takes great pride in the winery's very fine wines.*

"*Making good wine is a skill. Fine wine is an art.*

— Robert Mondavi

Crown Valley Port House

Crown Valley Port House

25795 Highway N
Clarksville, Missouri 63336
(573) 242-3695
www.crownvalleywinery.com

Owner: Joe Scott Senior
Winemaker: Daniel Alcorso
Region: Central
Established: 2006

Crown Valley Port House is a unique addition to the Missouri wine industry. Although the Port House is an offshoot of Sainte Genevieve's Crown Valley Winery, it seems worlds away from the hustle and bustle of the impressive and popular Winery, while still maintaining the same high standards that the Crown Valley name has come to stand for.

The Port House is located inside the private resort of Tievoli Hills in Clarksville, a historic, Mississippi River town about an hour northwest of Saint Louis, just off Highway N. Clarksville, famous for the bald eagles that make it their home each winter, is a delightful town with a thriving artistic community.

Tievoli Hills, a comfortable, 178-acre getaway, is surrounded on all sides by thousands of acres of undeveloped, natural beauty and fits right in with Clarksville's relaxed pace of life. The private resort is complete with a country-club theme and features such amenities as a restaurant, a clubhouse, tennis courts, a miniature golf course, an outdoor swimming pool, and a marina. None of these are its finest feature though.

Within the beautiful private resort is the Port House, which opened in September 2006. The early steps of Port production take place at Crown Valley Winery, which include the making of wine followed by its fortification using distilled grape spirits to boost the alcohol content. Then, when the fortified wine is ready to begin the aging process, it is sent to the Port House. It is not until after this final step that the fortified wine is ready to be bottled as Port and enjoyed by wine lovers everywhere. Visitors are encouraged to take a tour of the facility and see the barrel- and bottle-aging Port up close.

No visit would be complete without tasting the spectacular final product of so much skill, hard work, and patience. The Port House features a luxurious tasting bar, where visitors can sample its Port, as well as many other Crown Valley wines. The tasting room, which incorporates gorgeous hardwood floors, walls decorated with intricate woodwork, and large windows overlooking the outdoor patio, provides the perfect place to sit back and enjoy that favorite bottle picked out after a wine tasting.

Visitors to the Port House can also enjoy lunch at the bistro, pick up a book, shirt, or other souvenir in the gift shop, or watch a movie, wineglass in hand, in the newly-finished custom movie theater. As another option, the outdoor patio provides a lovely setting to sip a glass of wine, especially at sunset, and visitors can even enjoy live music there on weekends from April through October. Only a short drive from home, yet so many miles from the worries of life, a trip to the Port House is the perfect getaway, whether for several days or just several hours.

ABOVE: The Port House's bistro serves up wonderful snacks and meals that pair very nicely with its wines.

BELOW: Visitors can sample the Port and many other award-winning Crown Valley wines in the luxurious tasting room.

BELOW: The newly-finished custom movie theater is a wonderful way to relax after a day of wine tasting.

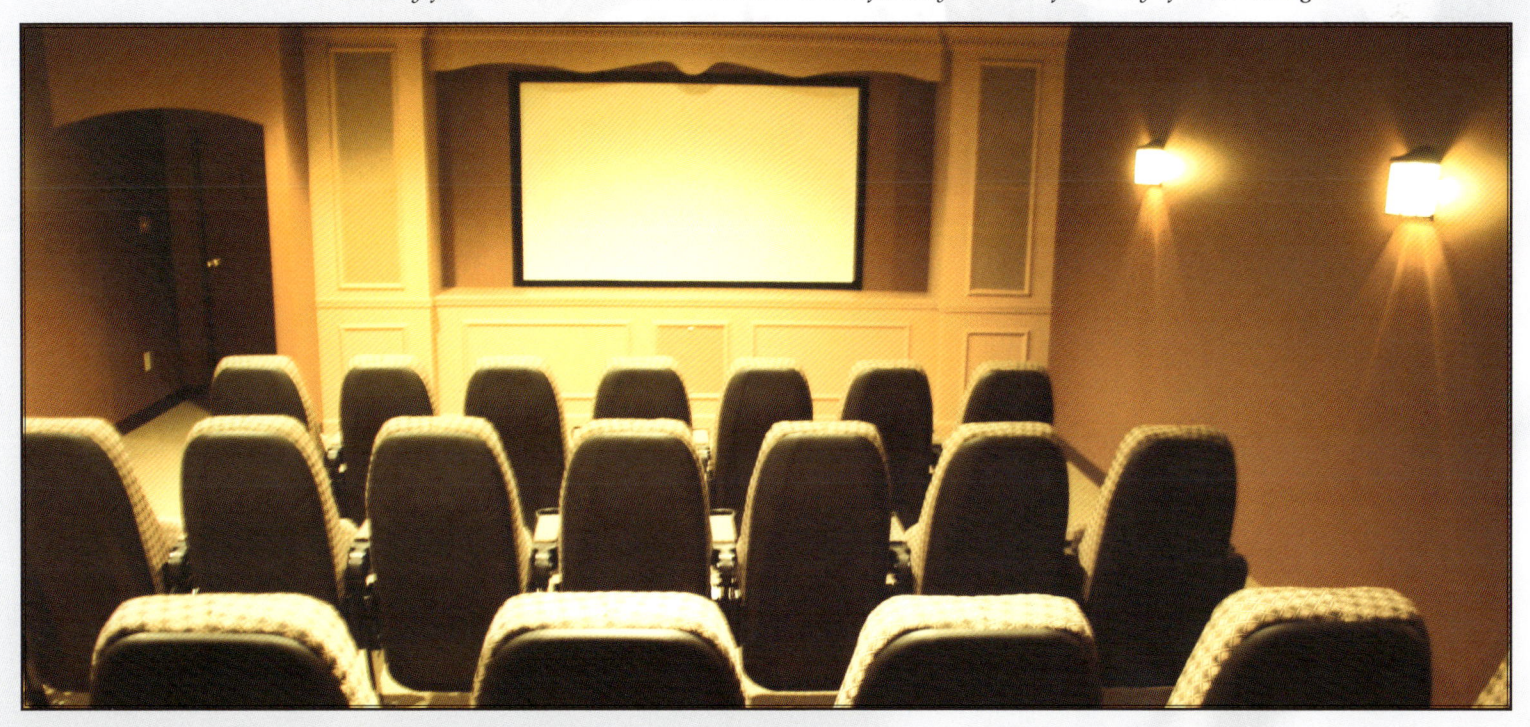

"*The aim of Port is to give you a good and durable hangover, so that during the next day you should be reminded of the splendid occasion the night before.*

— George Mikes

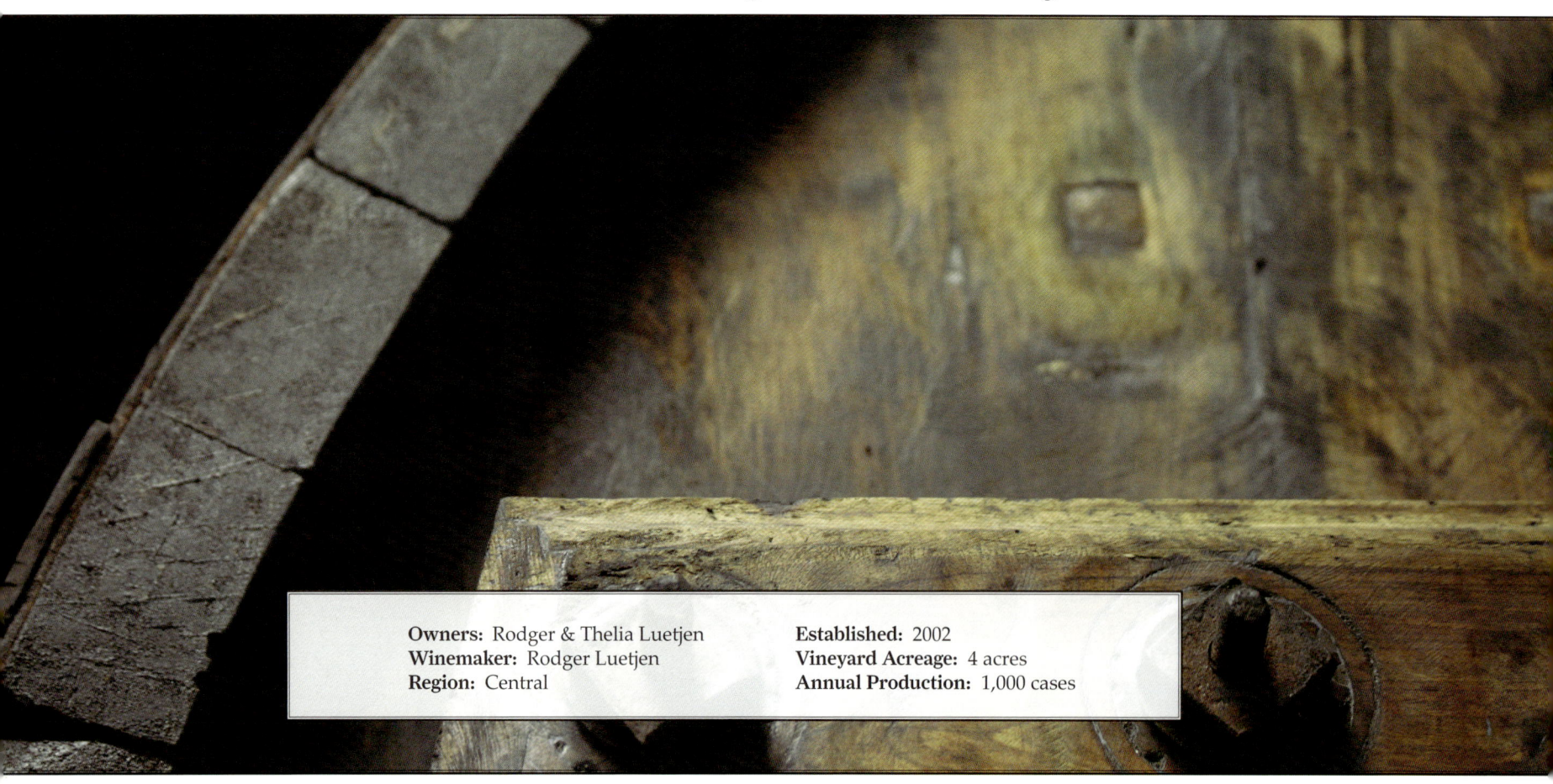

Eichenberg Winery

Owners: Rodger & Thelia Luetjen
Winemaker: Rodger Luetjen
Region: Central

Established: 2002
Vineyard Acreage: 4 acres
Annual Production: 1,000 cases

Eichenberg Winery owner and winemaker Rodger Luetjen's love for vineyards extends all the way back to his childhood. When he was a boy, his grandfather owned a winery, and Rodger and his adventurous cousins loved to play in the "castles, mazes, tunnels, and fortresses" that they discovered between the rows of grapevines. At the time, the fact that the grapes were of the same varietals as those found in his ancestors' northern Germany did not interest Rodger much. Instead, he preferred to concern himself with merely eating the grapes, though this frequently gave him an upset stomach.

Years later, after Rodger and his wife, owner Thelia Luetjen, became grandparents, his childhood memories came flooding back to him. Wanting his grandchildren to be able to have the same experiences that he had as a boy, Rodger started planting grapevines in 1996. Four years and countless hours of hard work later, the Luetjens took the next logical step for any vineyard owners, trying their hand at winemaking.

The couple loved producing their first vintage of wine so much that they bought more land and planted even more vines, for a total of four acres of vineyard with almost a dozen different grape varietals. Needing a larger winemaking facility, the Luetjens purchased a building in 2001 in downtown Cole Camp. The building dates back to the turn of the 20th century, when it served as a blacksmith's shop, and it has since been nominated for the National Register of Historic Places. The Luetjens selected the name Eichenberg, loosely translated from German to "Oak Hills," to reflect both the landscape around Cole Camp and their German heritage.

Eichenberg prides itself on offering visitors a warm, welcoming, family atmosphere. In fact, the Luetjens even keep a photograph of their own family next to the tasting counter and happily tell family stories when asked about it. One of the stories may be about how members of their family have pitched in to help produce Eichenberg's nine delicious wines, such as its Norton or Seyval, or one of its unique blends.

To complement its fine wines, visitors are welcome to purchase snack trays from the winery or even have a pizza delivered directly to the winery by Calgaro's Pizza. Eichenberg invites its visitors to enjoy a bottle of wine in the sunny wine garden or in the shade of the covered shelter.

After a relaxing day of wine tasting, visitors can stroll the streets of downtown Cole Camp and browse its several gift and antique shops, all of which are within walking distance of Eichenberg. For those interested in taking a peaceful and soothing weekend vacation to the area, the winery will help visitors make reservations at a local bed and breakfast.

Eichenberg welcomes visitors of all ages, whether they are old enough to enjoy its fantastic wines or young enough to play among the grapevines in the vineyard. At Eichenberg, they are all as good as family.

Eichenberg Winery

103 North Olive
Cole Camp, Missouri 65325
(660) 668-3511
www.eichenbergwinery.homestead.com

LEFT: Visitors to Eichenberg's tasting room get the opportunity to sample a variety of excellent wines.

RIGHT: Guests are always smiling while enjoying a fantastic bottle of Eichenberg wine.

WINE LIST

RED:

Baco Noir, Concord, Norton, & Triple Creek

WHITE:

Elvira, Eve's Sin, Liebersaft, Seyval, & Weiswein

BLUSH:

Rosawein

Quickly, bring me…wine, so that I may wet my mind and say something clever.

— Aristophanes

Grey Bear Vineyards & Winery

Owners: David & Marschall Fansler
Winemakers: David Fansler & Dino Diaz
Region: Central

Established: 2004
Vineyard Acreage: 8 acres
Annual Production: 2,200 cases

As any wine enthusiast knows, a full winery experience encompasses much more than just wines. Grey Bear Vineyards & Winery certainly provides visitors with a complete experience, offering fine wines, a fun atmosphere, and one of the most unique and interesting winery buildings in Missouri.

In 1990, owner and winemaker David Fansler, a Colorado restaurant owner at the time, planted grapevines on the small Colorado farm that he and his late wife owned. Three years later, when the vines began to produce grapes, the couple closed the restaurant and opened a winery to begin making wines from the grapes. In 2001, after the death of his wife, David married Marschall, and the couple pursued the expansion of their Colorado winery. Frustrated with high prices and red tape, the Fanslers began looking elsewhere in the country for the perfect new location for their winery. After unsuccessful searches in Oregon, New Mexico, and Wyoming, the couple drove 17 hours to Missouri and fell in love with the property on which Grey Bear now sits. The couple practically moved their Colorado winery to Grey Bear's current location in Stover.

No strangers to the nontraditional (their wedding had an 1880s-cowboy theme), the Fanslers decided to build a truly-unique building to house Grey Bear. After thoroughly researching numerous design possibilities, attending a three-day training seminar on the design and construction of a Deltec structure, and finally deciding on the Deltec circular-house design, the Fanslers began construction of the winery.

Its basement, which contains the winemaking facility, tasting room, and gift shop, was constructed using seven inches of reinforced concrete sandwiched

—43—

between three-inch layers of insulation to reduce heating and cooling costs. Originally, the Fanslers lived in the upper level of the building, enjoying a 360-degree view that included the vineyard and lush countryside. After careful thought though, they decided to renovate the area, making it a restaurant and microbrewery.

In addition to its impressive winery, visitors are delighted by Grey Bear's many award-winning wines made from Cabernet Sauvignon, Cayuga, Chambourcin, Concord, Marechal Foch, Muscat Canelli, Norton, Seyval Blanc, and Vignoles grapes. The winery can accommodate up to 40 visitors, welcomes small, private gatherings and parties with advanced reservations, and hosts an annual harvest supper, where visitors spend the day picking grapes. In the evening, they then enjoy a meal complete with wines made from the same varietal of grapes picked earlier in the day.

With plans already underway for a rental house onsite and a wind-generated power system, Grey Bear will surely always be one of Missouri's most unique wineries.

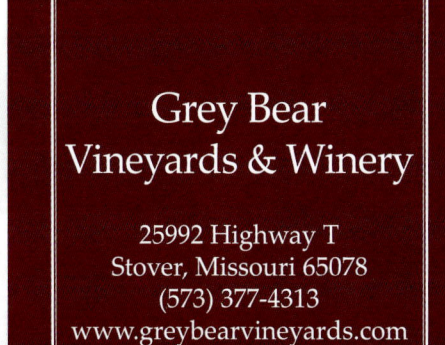

Grey Bear Vineyards & Winery

25992 Highway T
Stover, Missouri 65078
(573) 377-4313
www.greybearvineyards.com

LEFT: Each of Grey Bear's reds is fermented in a finely-crafted, American-oak barrel.

BELOW: After only a few years of winemaking, each oak barrel is retired to one of various permanent positions throughout the property.

BELOW: Owner Marschall Fansler loves serving visitors from behind the winery's beautiful tasting-room bar.

And Noah began to be a husbandman, and he planted a vineyard.

— Genesis 9:20

Indian Creek Winery

Owners: John & Sheila Osbourne & Rusty Osbourne

Winemaker: Sheila Osbourne

Region: Central

Established: 2007

Vineyard Acreage: 1 acre

Annual Production: 750 cases

Indian Creek Winery

39799 Highway 24
Monroe City, Missouri 63456
(573) 735-1135
www.indiancreekwine.com

Indian Creek Winery may be one of Missouri's newest wineries, but that has not stopped it from creating a wine list to rival some of the state's much larger and older wineries. Owners John and Sheila Osbourne, along with son Rusty Osbourne, pride themselves on the winery's wide selection of flavorful wines, including those made from many select Missouri grape varietals.

Although Indian Creek did not sell its first bottle of wine until 2007, the property's history goes back much farther. The historic farmhouse, which still stands as a reminder of the property's rich past, was built in 1917 for Charles and Pinkie Elzea. The Elzeas raised an interesting combination of Oxford sheep and lilies on their farm. Fortunately for wine lovers, the property eventually passed into the hands of the Osbournes.

Indian Creek is well known and well loved locally, and its popularity is sure to continue to spread with time. In addition to making Norton, Seyval, and Vignoles wines, Indian Creek produces a fantastic, jewel-toned blackberry wine and several original blends. The winery also makes a sacramental wine that is used in local church services. In order to keep up with the demand for its wines, Indian Creek plans to expand both

ABOVE: Indian Creek is known and loved for its rich, beautiful vegetation.

its production and its wine list very soon. In particular, several new blends and a sweet peach wine are already in the works, each of which will be great for visitors to enjoy on the winery's outdoor patio.

Indian Creek's visitors have the opportunity to enjoy more than just delightful wines though. The winery sells handmade baskets and other gifts crafted by the winery's Amish neighbors and fresh fruits and vegetables grown on the property's farm. Visitors can also enjoy freshly-baked treats made in the winery's kitchen and, during the holidays, candies and other special holiday treats.

Although Indian Creek is only a short drive off the beaten path, its tranquility and beauty make it feel worlds away. The combination of the winery and several nearby attractions provides plenty to justify an entire weekend getaway to the area. After a pleasant wine tasting at Indian Creek, visitors can head just 20 miles northeast to Hannibal and pay a visit to the boyhood home of Samuel Clemens, better known as Mark Twain. Mark Twain Cave, which the famous writer frequently explored as a boy, is also worth a stop, and Cannon Dam, located off Mark Twain Lake, offers breathtaking views and excellent fishing and bird watching. With a wide variety of fine wines and so many other unique and interesting attractions in the area, Indian Creek is well worth a visit.

ABOVE: Owner and winemaker Sheila Osbourne loves serving up both welcoming smiles and exquisite wines.

LEFT: Indian Creek's Strawberry Wine is not to be missed.

If God forbade drinking, would He have made wine so good?

— *Cardinal Richeleu*

Les Bourgeois Vineyards & Winery

Owner: Curtis Bourgeois
Winemaker: Cory Bomgaars
Region: Central

Established: 1985
Vineyard Acreage: 35 acres
Annual Production: 40,000 cases

Although Les Bourgeois Vineyards and Winery's original owner, Doctor Curtis Bourgeois Senior did not envision a winery on the property when he purchased it more than three decades ago, the beautiful property perched prominently atop a bluff overlooking the Missouri River, just outside of historic Rocheport, is now home to Missouri's third-largest winemaking operation. The winery's incredible growth has been necessary to accommodate wine lovers' ever-increasing demand for its wonderful wines throughout not just the state, but the entire Midwest.

Curtis Senior and his wife, Martha Bourgeois, bought the 15-acre property in 1974. After making some minor renovations, the couple and their four children moved into a small A-frame structure on the property, where they lived for two years during the construction of their new house. While living there, the Bourgeois family planted a small vineyard on a hilltop near the A-frame structure. This first vineyard was not planted to provide grapes for winemaking, but rather for beautification of the property. Fortunately for wine enthusiasts, it quickly began to serve both purposes.

When the grapevines first began producing grapes, the family tried its hand at winemaking. Using the grapes from the first significant harvest and the winemaking facility at a Rolla winery, they made 200 cases of a red wine. The couple's oldest child, current owner Curtis Bourgeois, who had already reached young adulthood, quickly recognized that the grapes from the property were of astounding quality, and in 1986, he took the reins of the Bourgeois family's winemaking operation. That summer, he and the rest of the family worked together to renovate the A-frame structure again, this time adding a sales counter, a food preparation area, and coolers. Once they completed the renovation, Les Bourgeois placed a few modest advertisements in local newspapers and opened for business. Its single varietal that year was an overwhelming hit. By October, only two months after opening its doors, the winery's entire first vintage of Jeunette Rouge had already been sold. The very next year, Les Bourgeois increased its production and added two new varietals to its wine list, but this only delayed the inevitable by another month, as it sold every bottle of wine that it produced that year by November.

Rather than continuing to produce its wines at the Rolla winery, Les Bourgeois moved its winemaking process not just closer to home, but actually to the

Les Bourgeois Vineyards & Winery

12847 West Highway BB
Rocheport, Missouri 65279
(573) 698-2133
www.missouriwine.com

ABOVE: Today, the vineyards at Les Bourgeois provide high-quality grapes and beautiful views, especially at sunset.

RIGHT: The 6,000-square-foot Blufftop Bistro was designed to let visitors enjoy the wonderful view of the Missouri River.

ABOVE: Enjoying a glass of Les Bourgeois wine with a delicious snack basket is the perfect afternoon delight.

ABOVE: The Blufftop Bistro's patio, with its magnificent view, is a popular location for wedding ceremonies.

ABOVE: The winery's A-Frame Outdoor Winegarden among visitors seeking a relaxing atmosphere, unparalleled view, and great bottle of wine.

home for the next four years. The grapes were crushed in the driveway, the wines were fermented in the garage, and the bottling line was set up in the kitchen and had to be dismantled and stored between runs. By its sixth year in operation, Les Bourgeois outgrew the Bourgeois home. In 1991, the winery purchased seven acres of property near I-70's Rocheport exit. On the land sat a 10,000-square-foot brick building that allowed Les Bourgeois to expand its operation to produce more than 8,000 cases annually.

The next addition took place in 1994, when Les Bourgeois purchased a 15-acre piece of property for its Blufftop Bistro. Stephen Bourgeois designed the magnificent, 6,000-square-foot structure, which features a timber frame, an open layout, and large windows providing a view of the Missouri River below, and construction was completed in 1996. Consistently voted "Boone County's Best Place to Take Out-of-Town Guests," the Blufftop Bistro delights visitors year round with its menu featuring signature house-smoked meats, fresh seafoods, hearty pastas, and only the finest produce, some of which is even grown in the winery's own garden.

The wine list at Les Bourgeois is as impressive as the view from its Blufftop Bistro. Its ever-growing list includes the Brut Sparkling Wine, Concord, Fleur Du Vin, Jeunette Rouge, LaBelle, Pink Fox, Port, Premium Claret, Riverboat Red, Riverboat White, and Solay. Les Bourgeois also features an annual Collector's Series of three new and unique wines, with labels designed using the winning artwork from its Wine Label Art Competition. The wines in its Collector's Series are made in small batches from the winery's best grapes, so as to focus on quality rather than quantity, and are considered to be the highest-quality wines released each year.

Visitors find the winery's rustic yet comfortable A-Frame Outdoor Winegarden to be the perfect place for enjoying Les Bourgeois wines. After selecting a bottle of wine in the A-frame, visitors can retire to one of the many gazebos and picnic tables throughout the tiered, partly shaded Winegarden. For those who enjoy a delicious snack with their wines, Les Bourgeois also provides the perfect complement in its sausage, cheese, apple, and bread basket. While the wines and snacks delight any visitor, it is the view from the A-Frame Outdoor Winegarden that truly takes breaths away. With a view similar to that from the winery's Blufftop Bistro, visitors can easily spend several hours just taking in its beauty.

Les Bourgeois offers a unique combination of rural quaintness and convenient accessibility. Located just one mile off I-70, halfway between Kansas City and Saint Louis, the winery is a popular destination for visitors of all types, especially for those drawn to Rocheport by its fine antique shops, world-class bed and breakfasts, and access to the Katy Trail. Les Bourgeois is a truly unique and wonderful experience for any wine lover.

ABOVE: The A-frame that once served as the Bourgeois-family home now serves up wines and snacks to visitors enjoying the view from the winery's casual A-Frame Outdoor Winegarden.

BELOW: The wine list at Les Bourgeois is as impressive as the view.

We could in the United States make as great a variety of wines as are made in Europe, not exactly of the same kinds, but doubtless as good.

— Thomas Jefferson

Little Hills Winery & Restaurant

Owners: David & Tammy Campbell
Winemaker: Phil Graczyk
Region: Central

Established: 1982
Vineyard Acreage: 10 acres
Annual Production: 10,000 cases

For visitors who enjoy a taste of history with their wines, Little Hills Winery & Restaurant in historic Saint Charles is well worth a visit.

The property's ownership dates back to 1805, just one year after the arrival of Lewis and Clark to the area, when it was purchased for a mere $1,500. The property was first home to a pharmacy, but later, during Prohibition, was used as part of a whisky-bootlegging operation. Following the repeal of Prohibition, a tavern opened on the property and was in business until owners David and Tammy Campbell purchased it for their winery.

Little Hills' vineyard was planted in 1980, and wine production began soon after, in 1982. At that time, the production process took place in Augusta, Eolia, and Saint James. In 2005 though, Little Hills began to produce and bottle its own wines in Saint Charles.

Little Hills' visitors find beauty everywhere they look. The winery's historic caverns create a nostalgic, Old-World feel, with wood barrels fermenting delicious wines stacked neatly against the brick-lined walls. The winery's caverns are complemented nicely by the elegant woodwork found in the restaurant. More impressive than the restaurant's woodwork is its menu, which includes dishes such as Goat Cheese Salad for lunch and Lobster Ravioli and Chicken Piccata for dinner. To help visitors, Little Hills recommends a wine for each entrée. Lunch and dinner are served seven days a week, and a breakfast buffet is even offered on the weekend.

Also available seven days a week, in the gift shop as well as the restaurant, is the opportunity for visitors to taste each Little Hills wine. The wine list features 20 wines, several of them award winning and all of them made from Missouri grapes. Some of the winery's more popular wines include the Catawba, Chardonel, Concord, Seyval, Traminette, Vignoles, and last but not least,

Strawberry wines.

For those who prefer to enjoy wines in the great outdoors, Little Hills' outdoor garden is a sight to be seen. The garden features terraced ponds littered with stones and tiny waterfalls, as well as fireplaces and seating for up to 300 visitors. It is the perfect place to sit with wineglass in hand, relax, and let time gently drift by.

Before visitors return home, they can stop in Little Hills' gift shop, which boasts a large selection of wine accessories and custom gift baskets. With its beautiful winery and delicious wines and foods, Little Hills will surely delight any visitor

ABOVE: Little Hills' tranquil waterfall provides a soothing atmosphere for enjoying wines with family and friends.

LEFT: The winery's ivy-covered building invites guests to come inside for a glass of wine or an entire afternoon of fun.

Little Hills Winery & Restaurant

501 South Main Street
St. Charles, Missouri 63301
(636) 946-9339
www.littlehillswinery.com

Hardly did it appear, than from my mouth it passed into my heart.

— Guillaume Amfrye de Chaulieu,
upon first tasting wine

Native Stone Winery

Owners: Larry & Cara Stauffer
Winemaker: Larry Stauffer
Region: Central

Established: 2000
Vineyard Acreage: 12 acres
Annual Production: 1,000 cases

Located on an expansive 300-acre property along the Missouri River bluffs lies Native Stone Winery. The estate has been farmed by the Stauffer family since the 1960s and is named for the national, award-winning play "Native Stone," which was written by Jim Steerman and based on the lives of the Stauffer family's ancestors. While Meriwether Lewis and William Clark came to the area in 1804 on their way to the Pacific coast, visitors today come for Native Stone's rich history, great wines, handcrafted beers, beautiful scenery, and relaxing atmosphere.

In 1804, Lewis and Clark, leaders of the Corps of Discovery, explored the riverside of Native Stone while on the first American overland expedition to the Pacific coast. As they explored, they came across a large rock formation, Bull Rock, which they noted in their journals. In celebration of the Lewis and Clark Bicentennial, Native Stone opened a trail for visitors to take a beautiful, one mile hike to Bull Rock, complete with signage chronicling the Corps of Discovery's trip through Missouri.

An easy walk for all ages, the trail offers the perfect opportunity to spend time with friends and family while viewing some of the better things that nature has to offer, such as turtles, ducks, geese, wild turkey, deer, and even

ABOVE: Native Stone has something for every visitor.

eagles soaring over the river in the winter. The trail can be hiked in one hour, but visitors typically find it too beautiful to rush through. When returning, visitors find Native Stone's tasting room, gift shop, and restaurant located in a newly remodeled, 19th-century farmhouse. The restaurant seats 60 inside and can accommodate more than 100 on the covered decks, sunny patios, and manicured lawns. The farmhouse also houses the Stauffers' Bull Rock Brewery, which always has several unique, handcrafted brews on tap.

While the brewery sells wonderful beers, visitors come from near and far for Native Stone's remarkable wines. Among their favorites are its 2003 Norton Port, a Missouri Wine Competition gold medal winner, and its 2004 Estate-Bottled Chambourcin, a bronze medal winner at the Competition. Since 2004, Native Stone has won 13 wine awards throughout the state, which is quite impressive for such a relatively young winery. With a selection of seven wines ranging from dry to dessert, visitors never have a problem finding a favorite.

Rich history, great wines, handcrafted beers, beautiful scenery, and relaxing atmosphere: Native Stone truly does have it all.

Native Stone Winery

4301 Native Stone Road
Jefferson City, Missouri 65109
(573) 584-8600
www.nativestonewinery.com

ABOVE: A great deal of hard work goes into every bottle of Native Stone wine.

RIGHT: The winery is home to Bull Rock Brewery, offering visitors a wide selection of wines and beers.

The wine in the bottle does not quench thirst.

— George Herbert

Phoenix Winery & Vineyards

Owner: Guenther Heeb
Winemaker: Guenther Heeb
Region: Central

Established: 2000
Vineyard Acreage: 10 acres
Annual Production: 1,300 cases

Many of Missouri's fine wineries boast rich German histories. Few, however, bring visitors as close to an authentic German experience as Phoenix Winery & Vineyards, located just outside of Owensville. Set peacefully at the end of a humble driveway in the partial shade of old, majestic trees, Phoenix is the creation of German-born owner and winemaker Guenther Heeb, who proudly offers a taste of his homeland.

For more than two centuries, the Heeb family grew grapevines on its German land for the production of fine, traditional wines. When Heeb says that winemaking is in his family's blood, he is not exaggerating. Heeb himself was born and raised in the renowned German winemaking region of the Rhine River, where he learned the customs and skills of his ancestors. Because he could not resist the pull of the enduring family tradition or the desire to usher in a new age of Heeb-family wines, he opened Phoenix in 2000 after immigrating to central Missouri.

Phoenix calls upon time-tested European traditions in crafting each of its wines. Its reds include the robust Draker-Steingarten, mellow Valiant, and mountain-berry-flavored Pink Passion. The winery also offers two wonderful blush blends in its semi-sweet Schiller and dry, delicate Draker Rosé. Finally, Phoenix's famous whites range from the crisp, dry Edelweiss to the sweet, fruity Himmels-Troepfchen, which proves true to its name, translating to "Droplets from Heaven" in German.

A winding gravel road gives visitors a picturesque tour of the full, leafy grapevines in Phoenix's vineyards, and in warm weather, visitors can stop and enjoy a glass of Phoenix wine on the terraced patio, which offers a mix of shade and sun in a relaxed, outdoor setting.

Phoenix provides not only fine German-style wines, but also an authentic German dining experience. The comfortable yet refined dining room accommodates gatherings as large as 25, and the winery offers catering of its wonderful foods and wines for lunch or dinner. For the greatest experience, Phoenix has organized the Edelweiss Dining Club, a biweekly meeting of members who enjoy a buffet of fine German foods complemented by wonderful Phoenix wines.

Whether enjoying a glass of Phoenix wine on their very first visit or as members of the Edelweiss Dining Club returning for a regular gathering, visitors are sure to experience a passion for the finer things in life. Phoenix's authentic German food and delicious wines make it the perfect choice for any wine lover wanting to step outside the ordinary.

Phoenix Winery & Vineyards

1840 Highway 50
Owensville, Missouri 65066
(573) 437-6278
www.phoenixwinery.com

BELOW: There is a bit of history in every bottle of Phoenix wine.

Wine brings to light the hidden secrets of the soul.

— Horace

Stone Hill Winery

Owners: Jim & Betty Held, Jon Held, Patty Held, & Thomas Held

Winemakers: Dave Johnson, Shaun Turnbull, & Tavis Harris

Region: Central

Established: 1982

Annual Production: 1,000 cases

Stone Hill Winery always provides those visiting its Hermann location with Old-World hospitality and the charm of its underground cellars, magnificent views, and exciting events. Because life is sometimes just too hectic to experience all that the Hermann location has to offer though, Stone Hill has made special accommodations for its busy wine lovers. Conveniently located off Interstate 70 at Exit 175, halfway between Columbia and Saint Louis, Stone Hill's New Florence location is the perfect stop for any traveler or day tripper.

Stone Hill sparkling wines were first produced in Hermann in 1977, but because of their amazing quality, there became a need to expand production to keep up with the demand for them. In 1982, a new sparkling-wine production facility was opened in New Florence, offering visitors a convenient stop for wine tasting, lunch, shopping, and the opportunity to experience the fine art of traditional sparkling winemaking.

While Stone Hill provides visitors the same award-winning wines and juices, quality wine-related gift items, and gracious hospitality that its Hermann location is known and loved for, visitors will also find a mouth-watering selection of whole, country-cured hams; ham steaks; sausages; cheeses; and smoked turkey breasts.

Uniquely, Stone Hill offers one thing that its Hermann and Branson locations do not: a firsthand glimpse into the traditional 18th-century French method of Champagne making. During a fun and informative tour, visitors learn the secrets of Méthode Champenoise, the method by which the finest Champagnes and sparkling wines in the world are still made.

Under Méthode Champenoise, a specially-selected wine, called a cuvee, is carefully bottled with a precise amount of sugar and special yeast. Typically, Vidal is chosen as the cuvee. The bottling of these ingredients results in a secondary fermentation of the wine within the sealed bottles, which takes between three weeks and three months and creates the pressure and famous bubbles. Even after this secondary fermentation, the bottles must remain undisturbed for three years. It is during this aging process, called tierage, that the special flavor of bottle-fermented sparkling wine develops. After the aging process, the bottles are placed neck down in riddling racks. Every day, each bottle is given a gentle shake and turn until all of the yeast has settled into the neck of the bottle. Keeping the necks down, the bottles are then placed in a freezing unit until the necks are frozen, trapping the yeast sediment. At this point, the bottles are turned up and quickly opened, allowing the pressure to push out the ice and yeast, a process called disgorging, which when properly done, results in a clear sparkling wine. Finally, a precise amount of a sugar-and-water mixture, called dosage, is added, which determines the sweetness of the sparkling wine, and the bottles are quickly corked with the final Champagne cork, which is wired in place.

Stone Hill's Blanc de Blancs, French for "White of Whites," is a Brut-style sparkling wine, finished with a touch of sweetness, and its Brut Rosé is a blush sparkling wine made from a blend of Vidal and Chambourcin. Whether enjoying one of the magnificent sparkling wines made onsite or any other award-winning Stone Hill wine or juice, visitors will not find more quality wines in such a convenient location.

Stone Hill Winery

485 Booneslick Road
New Florence, Missouri 63363
(573) 835-2420
www.stonehillwinery.com

ABOVE: Stone Hill wines are renowned not just for their quantity, but for their quality.

LEFT: Stone Hill sparkling wines are the perfect choice for any occasion.

BELOW: The winery takes great pride in producing its sparkling wines using a traditional 18th-century French method called "Méthode Champenoise."

Alas, I am dying beyond my means.

— Oscar Wilde, as he sipped sparkling wine on his deathbed

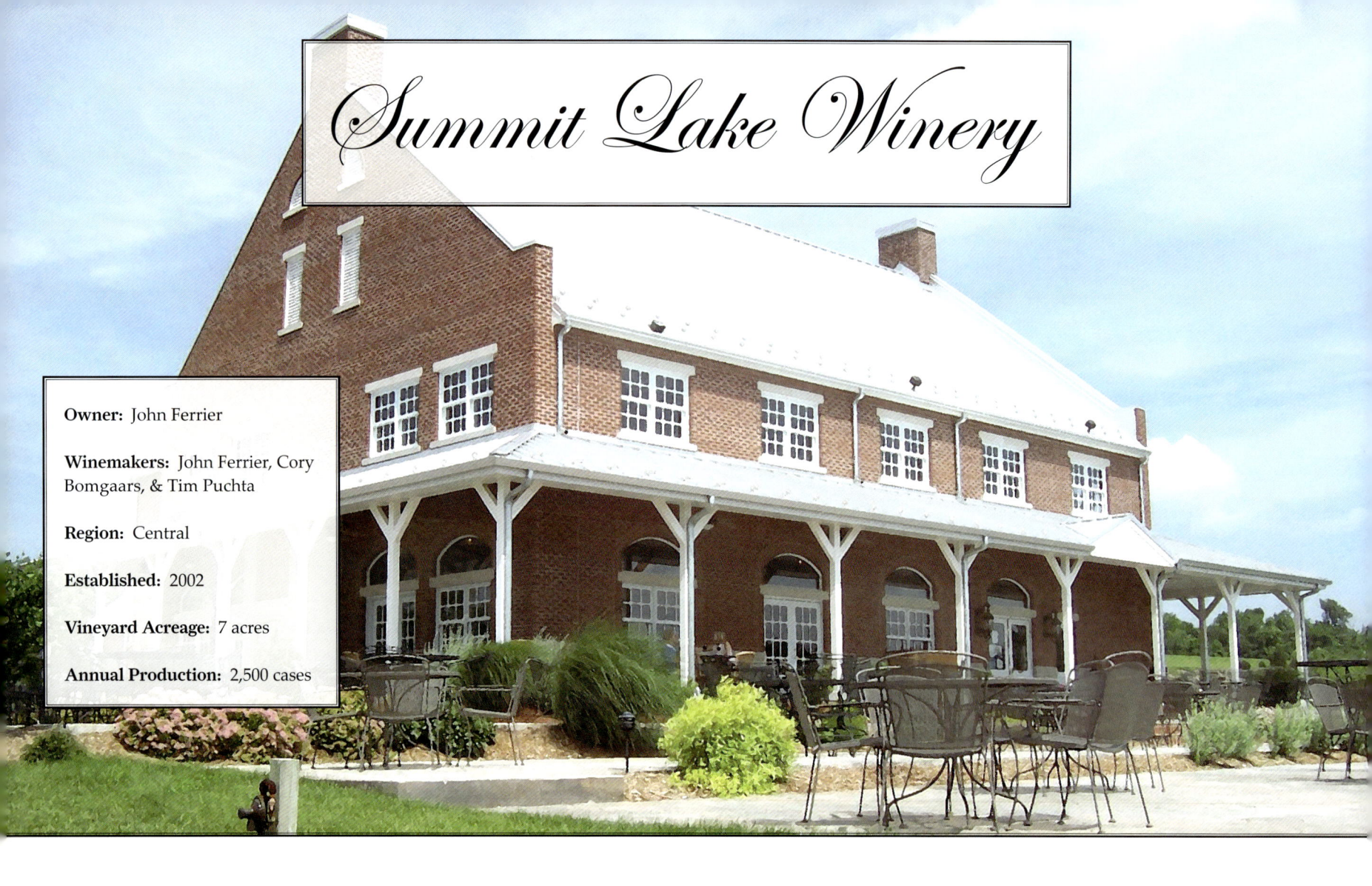

Summit Lake Winery

Owner: John Ferrier

Winemakers: John Ferrier, Cory Bomgaars, & Tim Puchta

Region: Central

Established: 2002

Vineyard Acreage: 7 acres

Annual Production: 2,500 cases

Summit Lake Winery, located in Holts Summit, is the product of a dream. Owner John Ferrier built the winery from the ground up, and he has continued to expand it over the years, even adding a second facility in Hartsburg, just as he has continued to dream.

Ferrier made his dream a reality in February 2002 when he established Summit Lake, which sits high on a bluff overlooking Highway 54 and the Missouri River, just north of Jefferson City. The winery was carefully planned to include a beautiful tasting room, an elegant bistro, banquet facilities, and plenty of outdoor seating on the garden terrace patio and the deck. Ferrier went further, however, in adding a number of fine amenities when constructing the winery, such as the beautiful landscaping outside and the warm, comforting fireplace inside.

Summit Lake's Bistro has helped earn the winery considerable attention, even being named *Mid-Missouri Mature Living* magazine's "Best Outdoor Dining Experience." The Bistro offers a wide selection of appetizers, salads, sandwiches, wraps, burgers, seafoods, and desserts, among other things, and visitors can enjoy both outdoor seating on the patio or deck in warm weather and indoor seating in the warmth of its fireplace in cooler weather. Additionally, the winery can accommodate and cater private parties, receptions, rehearsal dinners, conferences, and banquets as large as 200.

Summit Lake offers more than just a wonderful dining experience though. With 13 wines to its name, there is surely something for everyone. Summit Lake produces five single-varietal wines in its Chardonel, Missouri Port, Norton, Vidal Blanc, and Summit Mist, the last of which is made from Cayuga grapes. The winery also produces eight unique blends in its Callaway Bluff (Muscat and Vidal Blanc), Eberbach Red (Concord and Stark's Star),

Kingdom Bluff (Riesling, Seyval, and Vidal Blanc), Legend (Chambourcin and Norton), Lewis & Clark (Seyval, Vidal Blanc, and Vignoles), Saint Andrew (Norton and Saint Vincent), Saint Martin (Chambourcin and Norton), and So Blue (Riesling, Seyval, Vidal Blanc, and Vivant). To accommodate even those without a taste for wine, Summit Lake also offers a wide variety of foreign and domestic beers, as well as non-alcoholic sparkling grape juice.

In order to offer visitors a different wine-tasting experience, Summit Lake opened a second facility in Hartsburg. Although the two sites are only 15 minutes away from each other, they seem worlds apart, as the Hartsburg facility provides the ambiance of a slow-moving, Missouri River town hidden among beautiful countryside hills. Located only one block from the Katy Trail State Park, it provides the same delicious foods and fine wines as Summit Lake, with both indoor and outdoor seating.

Whether visiting Summit Lake in Holts Summit or its Hartsburg facility, visitors will surely enjoy their experience, just as the readers of the Jefferson City News Tribune have in voting it as their favorite winery in both 2005 and 2007.

Summit Lake Winery

1707 South Summit Drive
Holts Summit, Missouri 65043
(573) 896-9966
www.summitlakewinery.com

LEFT: Summit Lake's banquet center is casual enough for a social gathering yet formal enough for a wedding reception.

RIGHT: On Summit Lake's outside terrace, guests can enjoy a wonderful bottle of wine while savoring the beautiful view.

One not only drinks the wine, one smells it, observes it, tastes it, sips it and ... one talks about it.

— King Edward VII

The Eagle's Nest Winery

The Eagle's Nest Winery

221 Georgia Street
Louisiana, Missouri 63353
(573) 754-9888
www.theeaglesnest-louisiana.com

Owners: Karen & John Stoeckley

Winemaker: Cory Bomgaars

Region: Central

Established: 2001

Annual Production: 500 cases

Established in historic downtown Louisiana in 2001, The Eagle's Nest Winery offers everything that wine lovers could want in a winery: a tasting room where delicious wines are poured freely, a wine garden for enjoying a breath of fresh air with wineglass in hand, a bistro serving up great foods, a fun gift shop with plenty of souvenir and gift options, and beautiful overnight accommodations.

Located in the heart of downtown Louisiana, just two blocks from the Mississippi River, The Eagle's Nest is comprised of four adjacent buildings from the 1850s era. From the winery's outdoor patio, which is fully-enclosed and protected from the wind by 10-foot-high, 100-year-old stone walls, visitors can enjoy the company of the many eagles that soar overhead in the winter, helping give The Eagle's Nest its name.

Year round though, the winery happily offers wine tastings for a small cost, which include an etched The Eagle's Nest wineglass, and provides live weekend entertainment in its large dining hall. Uniquely, each of The Eagle's Nest's wines is named for a local point of interest or notable individual, and each of its labels is just the start of an interesting conversation.

The Eagle's Nest produces six intriguing wines: Buffalo Fort Norton, Mississippi River Rouge (a blend of Cabernet, Chambourcin, and other red wine grapes), Pikers Blush (made from Catawba grapes), Red Bud (a blend of Catawba and European-American hybrid red and white wine grapes), Rivera de Sel (a blend of Seyval, Vidal, and Vignoles grapes), and Sweet Louisiana Basye (a blend of Vidal and Muscat grapes). The Eagle's Nest wines are more than just intriguing though, as the winery has won medals for both its Buffalo Fort Norton and Sweet Louisiana Basye, and expects this list of medal winners to continue to grow with time.

The winery also carries a selection of wines from

Missouri's own Les Bourgeois Vineyards & Winery, three wines from Napa Valley's Smoking Loon (a Cabernet Sauvignon, Chardonnay, and Pinot Grigio), and a variety of French wines and Australian wines, so as to please the taste of any wine lover.

Visitors with an appetite for more than just wines can surely find a delicious snack or meal in The Eagle's Nest's bistro and restaurant. The winery proudly serves an Aged New York Strip, Veal Picatta, Slow-Roasted Saint Louis-Style Ribs in The Eagle's Nest's own bourbon barbeque sauce, Spiced Crusted Salmon, Lemon Peppered Catfish, a variety of soups, salads, and sandwiches, and much more. Early risers also enjoy The Eagle's Nest's offering of waffles, homemade biscuits and sausage gravy, giant cinnamon rolls, old-fashion oatmeal, and omelets made to order.

In addition to its wide selection of exquisite wines and foods, the winery also offers visitors overnight accommodations, which include seven private guestrooms, each with access to a spacious hot tub. Each guestroom is uniquely designed and beautifully furnished with modern amenities. With so much to offer, The Eagle's Nest is a true wine lover's delight.

ABOVE: The Eagle's Nest is located in the heart of Louisiana's historical downtown.

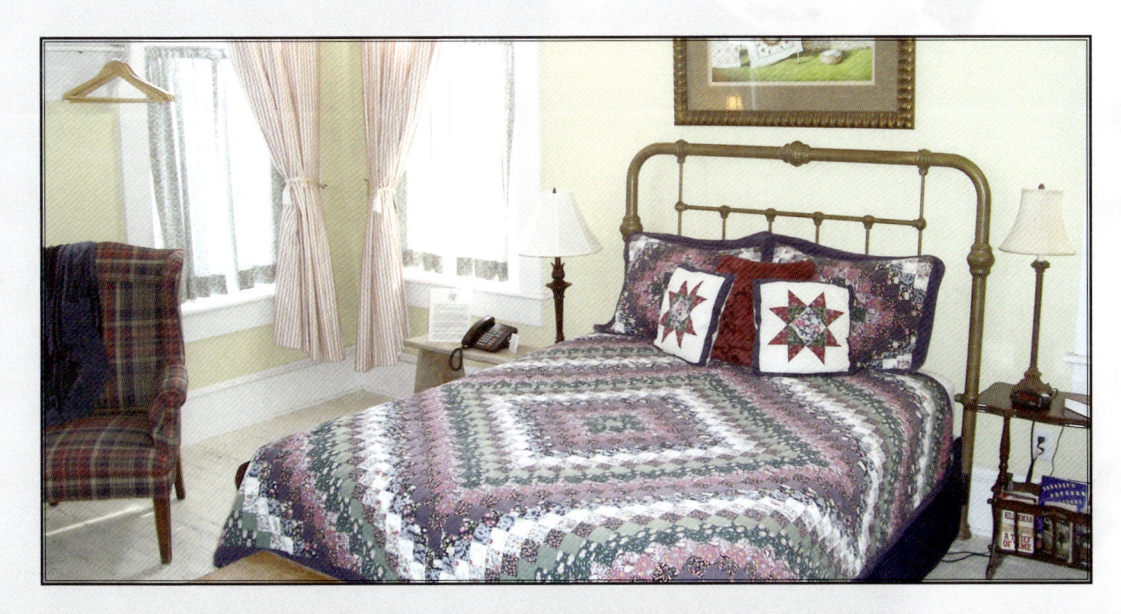

ABOVE: The winery's bistro is a great place for visitors to grab lunch.

LEFT: The Eagle's Nest provides visitors with luxurious overnight accommodations.

It is better for pearls to pass through the lips of swine than good wine to pass through the lips of the indifferent.
— Mark Luedtke

Hermann Region

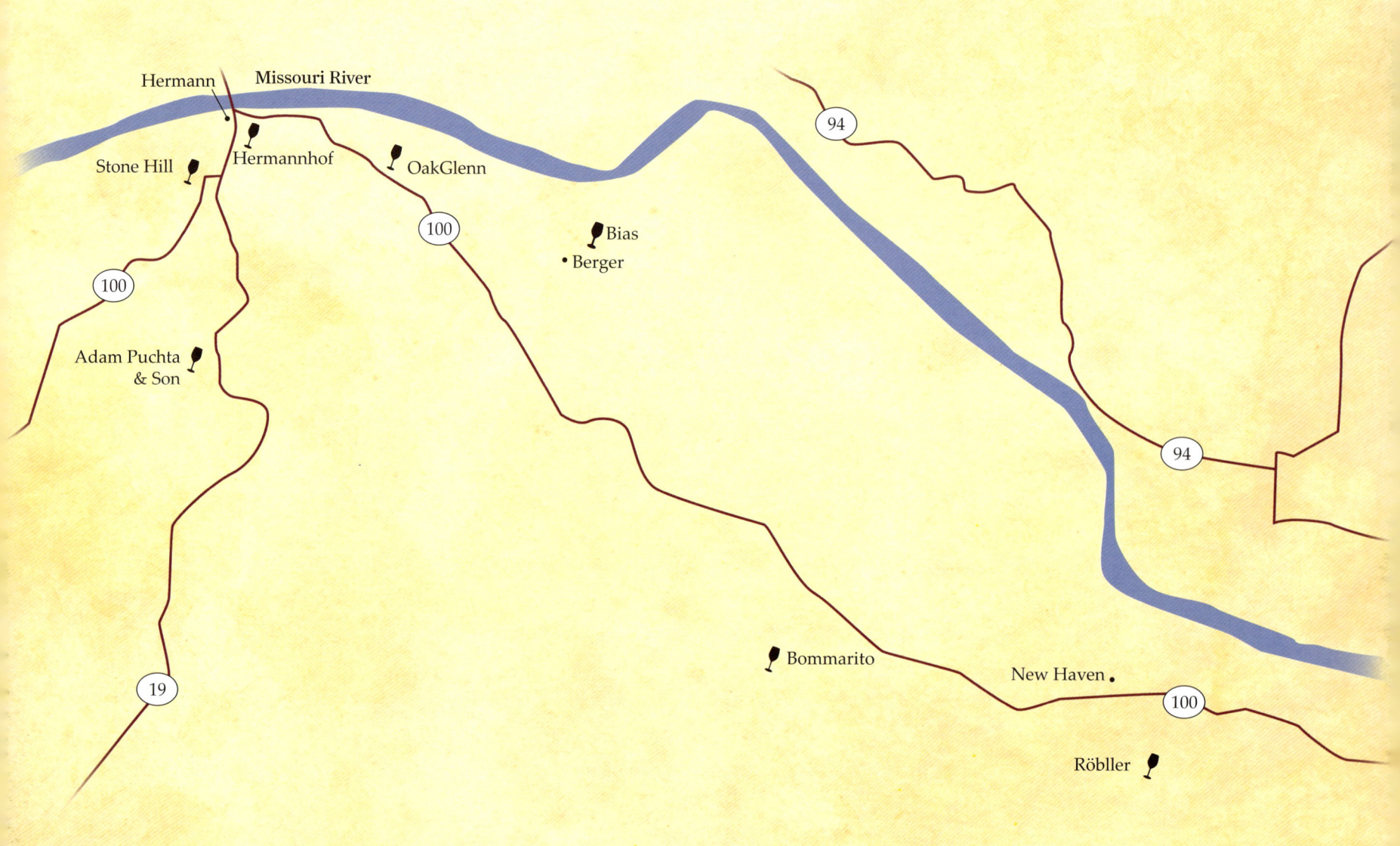

The Hermann region is an American Viticultural Area located on the southern side of the Missouri River in Gasconade County, about halfway between Saint Louis and the state capital of Jefferson City. The region is in a flood plain, which has led to alluvial soil deposits as deep as 30 feet. With growing conditions similar to those in southern and eastern Germany, it is no wonder that German immigrants found the region to remind them of their homeland and became its first settlers in the early 1800s. Not only did these Germans bring their traditions to the region, they also brought their skilled winemaking.

Wine production in the region grew rapidly, with Stone Hill Winery actually becoming the second-largest wine producer in the entire United States by the late 19th century. The region was not just known for the quantity of its wines, but also their quality. At the 1873 Vienna World Exposition, a Norton wine from the region was named "Best Red Wine of All Nations." In 1920, Prohibition quickly put an end to the region's wine industry though. Since its revival, the wineries of the region have returned to their glory, accounting for more than a third of the state's total wine production, and serve as the main attraction for visitors.

Visitors can also enjoy the region's beautiful landscapes, bed and breakfasts, museums, shops, galleries, and restaurants, many of which are among the region's more than 150 historic places on the National Register. For a fun, wine-tasting experience, visitors are encouraged to participate in any of the wine trails held throughout the year, including the Chocolate Wine Trail, Hermann Norton Wine Trail, Seven Hills of Hermann Bike Ride, Very Berry Wine Trail, and Holiday Fare Wine Trail. Whether visiting one of the region's wineries or other historic attractions, the Hermann region will delight any visitor.

Adam Puchta & Son Winery

Owner: Timothy Puchta
Winemaker: Michael Rouse
Region: Hermann

Established: 1990
Vineyard Acreage: 20 acres
Annual Production: 17,000 cases

Adam Puchta
& Son Winery

1947 Frene Creek Road
Hermann, Missouri 65041
(573) 486-5596
www.adampuchtawine.com

Located in the heart of central Missouri is Hermann, a picturesque, 19th-century town brimming with Old-World charm. Just a few miles southwest of this delightful town, on the banks of Frene Creek off Highway 100, lies Adam Puchta & Son Winery, the oldest family-farm winery in the state of Missouri. Its true uniqueness, however, lies in the fact that the same family has owned the property and winery since 1855.

The story of Adam Puchta & Son began on May 25, 1839, when 7-year-old Adam Puchta, along with his father, stepmother, older brother, and three stepsisters left the port of Hamburg, Germany for the United States. The family emigrated from Oberkotzau, Germany, a village in the northeastern corner of Bavaria near the Czech border, where Adam's father was a butcher, in search of a better life in the New World.

Upon the family's arrival at its destination, the German

ABOVE: Adam Puchta & Son's Bistro is open to visitors during festivals and wine trails.

settlement of Hermann, the family settled on a 40-acre tract of land north and adjacent to the property on which the winery now sits. Adam's father built a one-room log cabin and a small wine cellar with a press house above it, and in 1849, purchased an additional 40 acres, which is now part of the winery.

Rather than staying to work on the family farm, Adam left home for California in 1853 in search of gold. After striking it rich, he decided to return to Hermann. Using the riches he earned in California, he purchased the additional 40 acres of land from his father to begin his own farm, as well as his own family. Adam built a residence and began clearing the land for a vineyard and other crops. In 1855, he produced his first wines, using both wild grapes and grapes from his father's vineyard. This first vintage marked the start of a very fine family tradition.

Adam's early wine production took place in a small cellar under his residence. Within a short time, he realized the need for more storage and built a large, arched limestone cellar, which was quarried on the property from the same limestone used for the residence. Directly above the underground cellar, Adam built a press house and

ABOVE: Adam Puchta & Son produces some of Missouri's finest wines.

LEFT: The winery's production facility is the birthplace of so many great wines.

fermentation room. Today, visitors can still find the original cellar and press house on the property.

Over the next 30 years, both Adam's winery and his family grew. In the 1880s, Adam's son, Henry, joined him in the winemaking business, and Adam Puchta & Son Wine Company was born. Although the business expanded rapidly for the next few decades, it eventually came to a screeching halt.

When Prohibition went into effect in 1920, the Missouri wine industry, as well as the rest of the American wine industry, was all but killed off. Prohibition dealt a particularly devastating blow to the wine-based economy of the Hermann region. Grapevines were ripped out of the ground, and the former vineyards were converted to cropland. Nevertheless, the Puchtas continued to produce wine for family use from a few undestroyed grapevines and from elderberries, blackberries, and even dandelions.

In 1990, many years after the death of Prohibition, and as part of a strong revival of the Hermann and Missouri wine industries, father and son Randolph Puchta and Timothy Puchta realized a longtime dream by reopening Adam Puchta & Son to the public. Today, the winery is owned by Timothy, great-great-great grandson of the same Adam Puchta who began making wine on the property almost 150 years ago. While the winemaking process has evolved considerably over the last century and a half, Timothy has gone to great lengths to preserve much of the original character of his distant relative's winery. In fact, visitors can still view the dual-stone, hand-operated grape crusher and two-person, screw wine press used by

ABOVE: Adam Puchta & Son wines have won countless state and national awards.

— 67 —

Adam to produce the property's first wines.

In order to create its highly-acclaimed wines though, Adam Puchta & Son uses only the most-modern winemaking equipment. Each piece is made of high-quality stainless steel, including the crusher, destemmer, hopper, auger, fermenting and storage tanks, pumps, filters, and automatic-bottling equipment. Using this state-of-the-art equipment, Adam Puchta & Son produces award-winning wines at the state, national, and international levels, especially its Vignoles, the only Missouri wine to be awarded one of thirteen prestigious Jefferson Cups in 2007. Adam Puchta & Son's other fine wines include three reds (Hunter's Red, Legacy, and Traminette), four whites (Adam's Choice, Chardonel, Seyval, and Vidal Blanc), two blushes (Blush and Rosé), two dessert wines (Misty Valley and Riefenstahler), and two fruit wines (Berry Black and Jazz Berry).

Visitors come to Adam Puchta & Son for more than just amazing wines. Guests can visit the tasting room for a sample of each of the winery's fine wines or browse the gift shop for that perfect souvenir. Whether just making a short stop while traveling the Hermann wine trail or taking a full day to enjoy all that Adam Puchta & Son has to offer, visitors will not be disappointed.

ABOVE: The friendly tasting room staff is always eager to assist visitors in selecting the perfect bottle of wine.

" *Wine rejoices the heart of man, and joy is the mother of all virtues.*

— *Johann Wolfgang*

Bias Vineyards & Winery

Owners: Kirk & Carol Grass
Winemaker: Kirk Grass
Region: Hermann

Established: 1980
Vineyard Acreage: 9 acres
Annual Production: 4,500 cases

Bias
Vineyards & Winery

3166 Highway B
Berger, Missouri 63014
(573) 834-5475
www.biaswinery.com

A distinguishing mark of the Missouri wine industry is the sense of community and common interests shared by both wineries and wine lovers alike. Nowhere else is this more apparent than at Bias Vineyards & Winery.

Jim and Norma Bias purchased the property in the late 1970s. At the time, five acres of Catawba grapevines grew on the land. The Biases expanded the vineyard by planting four additional acres of European-American hybrid vines and began a 20-year period of commercial winemaking there. Unfortunately, when Norma died in 1997, the winery's future was placed in jeopardy.

Over the next two years, Jim's daughter and son-in-law, Karen and Dennis Jay, helped run the winery. During that time, Dennis introduced the idea of adding a microbrewery to the property, and the owners began the process of obtaining the proper licenses. When Gruhlke's Microbrewery was finally built, it made Bias the first combined winery and microbrewery in Missouri and only the second in the entire United States.

Soon after though, the Biases decided to sell the property. Fortunately, current owners Kirk and Carol Grass, decade-long Bias customers, did not let the beer and winemaking legacy of the property die. They continued to produce the wines that they had enjoyed as long-time customers of the winery, but also created their own unique wines to add to the Bias wine list. Today,

— 69 —

Bias produces between 20 and 25 different beers, keeping four to six on tap.

Bias's extensive and exceptional wine list makes the winery special in its own right. Bias produces eight reds (Berger Red, Chambourcin, Chambourcin Reserve, DeChaunac, Fredonia, Jubilee Red, River Mist, and Victorian Red), seven whites (Jubilee White, Liebeswein, Norma's Best, Premium River View White, Riesling, Vignoles, and Weisser Flieder), four blushes (Holiday Weisser Flieder, River Bluff Rouge, Strawberry Weisser Flieder, and Sweet Ambrosia), and a wonderful ice wine for dessert (Frosty Meadow White).

Visitors enjoy Bias as much for its beauty as for its fine wines and beers. The stunning 67-acre property overlooks the Missouri River bottomlands and is home to gorgeous wooded hills and a serene pond spanned by a small bridge. The nine-acre vineyard is located just a few hundred feet from the winery and microbrewery and can be seen while seated on the outdoor, covered patio and through the windows of Bias's cozy, indoor Fireside Room. The Fireside Room features a large, stone, wood-burning fireplace and is great for enjoying any of Bias's many wines and beers. The room can comfortably accommodate up to 100 visitors and can be rented for private gatherings. Summer or winter, rain or shine, a visit to Bias is not to be missed.

ABOVE: In the summer, Bias's wooden pavilion hosts live entertainment for hours of wine, music, and fun.

BELOW: Bias uses the highest quality grapes to produce each of its wines.

"*Wine makes every meal an occasion, every table more elegant, every day more civilized.*
— Andre Simon

Bommarito Estate Almond Tree Winery

Bommarito Estate Almond Tree Winery

3718 Grant School Road
New Haven, Missouri 63068
(573) 237-5158
www.bommaritoestatewinery.com

Owner: Nick Bommarito
Winemaker: Nick Bommarito
Region: Hermann
Established: 2000
Vineyard Acreage: 11 acres
Annual Production: 1,000 cases

Located on a beautiful, 21-acre farm in rural New Haven, just east of Hermann, Bommarito Estate Almond Tree Winery is the newest addition to the popular Hermann Wine Trail. Although new to the wine trail, Bommarito Estate is far from unskilled in winemaking. In fact, the winery produces a wide range of outstanding wines. Its 2002 Red Port, for example, won "Best of Class" at the 2007 National Norton Wine Competition, the top award for a Norton Port.

In 1996, owner and winemaker Nick Bommarito planted the winery's first Norton and Saint Vincent grapevines on a hillside behind his New Haven home. The vineyard has since grown to approximately 11 acres and now also includes Vignoles and Chambourcin vines. An avid organic gardener, Bommarito prides himself on the quality of the winery's vineyard, as he believes that good wines are made in the vineyard, not in the barrel. With the help of his children, Bommarito cares for and nurtures the grapevines year round. In addition to the vineyard, the entire winery operation is family run. During the harvest, the Bommarito family tirelessly works together to complete every aspect of the winemaking process, from destemming the grapes to bottling the wines, and

— 71 —

on any given weekend, visitors are likely to run into several Bommaritos working throughout the winery.

Bommarito Estate's winemaking legacy began four years after its first Norton and Saint Vincent grapevines went into the ground, when the winery opened its doors to the public and sold its first bottle of wine. Today, Bommarito Estate's wine list features its Almond Tree Blush, Almond Tree Rosé, Chambourcin, French Oak Norton, Saint Vincent, Vignoles, and best-selling Almond Tree Red, a Norton-Saint Vincent blend. Additionally, the winery produces a new Norton Port each year, much to the delight of any visitor who has ever tasted one of its award-winning Ports.

Each Bommarito Estate wine is available to sample and purchase in the winery's new tasting room. The air-conditioned tasting room, which accommodates up to 30 visitors, offers a perfect escape from the heat on a hot summer day, and its fireplace provides the warmth of a roaring fire on a cool autumn evening. Visitors who love a breath of fresh air also enjoy the picturesque views of the hills and valleys surrounding Bommarito Estate while comfortably sipping a glass of wine in the outdoor seating area.

Because Bommarito Estate is a small winery, it sells every bottle of wine that it produces each year. As a result, the winery is considering an increase in its production capacity so that more wine lovers will have the opportunity to enjoy its remarkable, award-winning wines. Although the winery will surely see such changes as time goes by, one thing will always remain the same: Bommarito Estate's mission to provide visitors with a beautiful and serene retreat from the bustle of everyday life.

ABOVE: Bommarito Estate's award-winning Norton is sure to tantalize the palate of even those with the most refined taste for wine.

ABOVE: Visitors can step inside Bommarito Estate's tasting room for an air-conditioned retreat on those hot summer days.

" *Great wine is made in the vineyard, not in barrels. It starts from the soil and what God gives you each season.*

— *Nick Bommarito, Bommarito Estate owner and winemaker*

Hermannhof Winery & Vineyards

Hermannhof Winery & Vineyards

330 East First Street
Hermann, Missouri 65041
(573) 486-5959
www.hermannhof.com

Owners: Jim & Mary Dierberg
Winemaker: Paul LeRoy
Region: Hermann
Established: 1978
Vineyard Acreage: 52 acres
Annual Production: 17,000 cases

At Hermannhof Winery & Vineyards, vineyard manager, grape harvester, and winemaker alike are all partners in the winery's excellence. This unique dedication to a common lofty standard has resulted in decades of wines of unmatched quality. In fact, Hermannhof is America's only two-time winner of the prestigious Brown-Forman Trophy.

Hermannhof's story began long ago. In 1848, construction of Hermannhof, a brewery and winery at that time, began in the French section of Hermann. Due to its size and elaborateness, the construction of Hermannhof's beautiful arched stone cellars and brick superstructure, both of which are on the National Register of Historic Places, took four years to complete.

Initially, Hermannhof's winemaking represented only a small portion of the total production of the successful brewery and winery operation. By 1904 though, the Hermann area was producing over a million cases of wine annually, and most of this was made by small-scale winemakers, many of whom utilized Hermannhof's facilities. Less than two decades later, Prohibition brought wine production throughout Hermann, as well as the rest of the nation, to a screeching halt.

In 1974, however, more than half a century since

— 73 —

closing its doors, owners Jim and Mary Dierberg purchased Hermannhof and began its restoration. After four years of work on the winery, a search was made for the most-ideal site in the area for grape growing. Soil composition, microclimate, and historical data were gathered, and the University of Missouri-Columbia was even consulted. The search culminated the following year in the purchase of two large, connecting farms totaling 300 acres: an upper farm and a lower farm, both with ideal slopes and scenic views. The very next year, an impressive 50-acre vineyard was laid out over the land.

The lower farm was the Christopher Weber vineyard and farm, planted in 1837. While little else is known about Weber, history books tell that he was "a famed dairyman, vintner, and musician." The upper farm, also called Hermannhof's Little Mountain vineyard or the Ruediger vineyard, was also planted in 1837, but by Julius Ruediger, a famous grape grower of his day. His original stone-and-log vintner's cabin remains unchanged, with rows of vines radiating from it.

Every amazing Hermannhof wine begins in the winery's vineyards, where the soil and climate distinguish the vineyards as a couple of those rare pieces of the Earth capable of producing the finest wines. The upper vineyard is located on the high bluffs at the meeting point of the Gasconade and Missouri Rivers, and has one of the highest elevations and vertical drops along the Missouri River. The sloping terrain enables the grapes to capture the full power of the sun, while rising mists from the rivers below protect the vines from frost. The deep, well-drained Menfro soil allows each plant to send its roots deep into the soil, resulting in classic, structured wines that improve with age, delighting connoisseur and first-time taster alike.

Although Hermannhof produces 17,000 cases of wine annually, it remains dedicated to quality rather than

BELOW: *The Inn at Hermannhof and Haus Wineries provide visitors spacious, all-suite accommodations for a truly memorable experience.*

ABOVE: Hermannhof wines are barrel aged in its magnificent underground, stone cellar.

BELOW: At the winery's tasting room counter, guests are invited to sample from a wide range of award-winning wines.

quantity. Because turning grapes into wine is a natural process, the winery focuses on preserving the grapes' natural character and quality throughout the winemaking process. To do so, Hermannhof utilizes the latest equipment and methods and devotes unprecedented time and effort to its winemaking. This dedication to quality has enabled the winery to become America's only two-time winner of the highly regarded Brown-Forman Trophy, which it won for "Best New World White Wine." The winery has also won countless other awards.

Although attentive to quality, Hermannhof still produces a very-wide selection of amazing wines. With 15 wines on its wine list, most notably including its Chambourcin, Norton, Vignoles, and White Lady of Starkenburg, any visitor is sure to find a wine to delight his or her taste buds. For those looking for a unique treat, Hermannhof's Port, of which less than 150 cases are produced each year, is not to be missed.

Hermannhof has so much more to offer visitors than just world-class wines though. Visitors may want to step inside the winery's century-and-a-half-old brick-and-stone main building, which features a tasting room with multiple tasting counters, a delightful gift shop, a deli offering authentic German-recipe sausages and other delicious snacks, a lovely indoor seating area with a fireplace, a special cellar tasting room, and an outdoor courtyard with a patio and grape arbor.

Even more impressive are

Hermannhof's historic underground cellars, which are located directly beneath the main building and are accessible by a staircase just off the main tasting room. The 10 magnificent stone cellars are still utilized today for the aging of Hermannhof's premium wines. Both French- and Missouri-white-oak barrels help age the wines until they are ready to be brought out to delight wine lovers throughout the world.

For a truly memorable experience, Hermannhof invites its visitors to stay over for the night in a luxurious suite at either the Inn at Hermannhof or one of Hermannhof's six Haus Wineries. The Inn, which offers eight luxurious suites, is located in the heart of historic Hermann. The Haus Wineries have a collective 20 suites and are located on the winery's East Hill. Each Haus Winery was formerly a working winery, but has been beautifully restored to retain its 1800s character and appeal. Whether staying at the Inn or one of the Haus Wineries, visitors will be pampered with a full breakfast and spacious whirlpool bathtub, and may even request an in-suite massage. For those searching for the perfect location for a reception, wedding, or business meeting, Hermannhof also has several banquet halls capable of accommodating up to 300 guests.

With so much history and amazing quality wrapped up into one beautiful winery, visitors will surely find everything they are looking for at Hermannhof.

ABOVE: Able to accommodate up to 300, the beautiful Festhalle is the perfect location for a wedding or any other gathering.

BELOW: The view from Hermannhof's vineyard is blissful and awe inspiring.

Compromises are for relationships, not wine.

— Sir Robert Scott Caywood

OakGlenn Winery & Vineyard

Owners: Glenn & Carolyn Warnebold
Winemaker: Patrick Straatmann
Region: Hermann
Established: 1997

OakGlenn Winery & Vineyard

1104 OakGlenn Place
Hermann, Missouri 65041
(573) 486-5057
www.oakglenn.com

Originally called "Schauinsland," German for "Look into the Country," because of its spectacular views, OakGlenn Winery commands an unmatched view of the Missouri River, the winery's vineyard, and the beautiful rolling hills of mid Missouri. Unknown to many, OakGlenn sits on a site once owned by internationally-renowned viticulturist George Husmann, regarded as "The Father of the Missouri Grape Industry."

On April 16, 1997, owners Glenn and Carolyn Warnebold visited the beautiful property that is now home to OakGlenn. So overwhelmed by the spectacular view, they purchased the property the very next month and named it OakGlenn. The winery's name was inspired by both a large, majestic oak tree that marked the driveway entrance and the name of one of the winery's new owners. The oak tree has since been removed from the entrance, but its trunk can still be found today on its side with the name "OakGlenn" carved into it. This beautiful addition sits beside a hand-carved bust of Husmann to greet visitors arriving at the winery.

After purchasing the property, the Warnebolds spent the next year tirelessly landscaping the property and cleaning up the remnants of the vineyard that was planted there 150 years earlier by Husmann. At the time, they were unaware that the overgrown vines, the majority of which had been dead for years, were originally planted by Husmann himself in 1847. Not only were the Warnebolds pleasantly surprised when they learned of the fascinating history of the vineyard on their property, but they were delighted to find five rows of the Norton grapevines planted by Husmann still alive.

Today, OakGlenn's visitors can still enjoy their own small piece of the property's rich history by sampling the winery's highly acclaimed Red Port. This rich, sweet, red dessert wine with strong berry flavors is made each year using grapes picked from the same grapevines that Husmann planted in the early 1800s.

In Husmann's honor, OakGlenn proudly showcases a series of 16 large displays documenting Husmann's life and contributions to wine industries worldwide. The displays are located in a large gathering area on the second floor of The George Husmann Wine Pavilion. OakGlenn's tasting room and gift shop are located on the first floor of the Pavilion, and they allow visitors to sample each of the winery's delicious wines and purchase wonderful wine-related items.

Just outside the front doors of the Pavilion is a large, covered porch, where visitors can marvel at the fantastic view of the Missouri River while enjoying one of OakGlenn's many award-winning wines. Weather permitting, visitors can also head over to the winery's outdoor patio next to the Pavilion, where live musical entertainment is provided on most Saturdays throughout the summer. Whether visitors crave extraordinary wines, breathtaking views, or just great memories, OakGlenn provides an ideal setting.

ABOVE: OakGlenn is not only a Missouri winery, but a proud American winery.

ABOVE: Visitors can enjoy a fine glass of OakGlenn wine and a magnificent view at The George Husmann Wine Pavilion.

ABOVE: OakGlenn's visitors enjoy the same breathtaking views of the Missouri River that George Husmann enjoyed nearly two centuries ago.

WINE LIST

RED:	WHITE:	BLUSH:
Chambourcin	Chardonel	Blush
Countryside Red	Chardonel Oak	
Husmann's Heritage	Moonbeam Melody	DESSERT:
Norton	Silver Moon	Port Red
Riverview Red	Vidal Blanc	Port White
Saint Vincent	Wine Cellar Choice	Sweet Caroline

" *Wine makes daily living easier, less hurried, with fewer tensions and more tolerance.*

— Benjamin Franklin

Röbller Vineyard Winery

Owners: Robert & Lois Mueller
Winemaker: Robert Mueller
Region: Hermann

Established: 1988
Vineyard Acreage: 16 acres
Annual Production: 2,000 cases

Röbller
Vineyard Winery

275 Röbller Vineyard Road
New Haven, Missouri 63068
(573) 237-3986
www.robllerwines.com

Röbller Vineyard Winery's roots were planted when owners Robert and Lois Mueller began dabbling in winemaking in their Glendale home. Each fall, family and friends would gather in the Muellers' backyard to help crush grapes for fermentation before sampling the previous year's vintage. Through the years, the quality of the Muellers' wines improved to such a great degree that they thought it only made sense to open a winery and share their wines with the world.

On a sunny day in December 1987, the Muellers took their children on a country drive. The drive led them to New Haven and ended at a beautiful piece of property with a breathtaking view of the Missouri countryside. The property offered southward-facing slopes, which received sunlight all day long, great soil composition, and the proper grade for drainage, all ideal conditions for a productive vineyard. Without question, the Muellers knew that they had found the perfect location for their winery.

They spent the next several months designing the layout of the vineyard and were actually able to begin planting grapevines by mid spring. While waiting for the vines to begin producing grapes, the Muellers spent 1989 and 1990 building the winery and setting up the equipment to produce the winery's first vintage. All of this hard work set the stage for a great new tradition in the Missouri wine industry.

Since the production of Röbller's first vintage in 1990, the winery's tasting room has welcomed thousands through its doors each year and proudly displays an array of awards from state and national wine competitions, including the prestigious Missouri Governor's Cup received for its 1993 Norton. With more and more wine lovers tasting and wanting more of its high-quality wines, Röbller quickly realized the need for a larger vineyard to keep up with the demand for its wines. The vineyard has grown to 16 acres, and includes such grape varietals as Chambourcin, Norton, Saint Vincent, Seyval, Steuben, Traminette, Vidal, Vignoles, and Villard Noir. From these grapes, Röbller produces only premium wines, focusing on European-American hybrid varietals and European-style blends, while also making a wonderful Norton, which has become a favorite of many visitors for its balance of rich fruits and spices.

Röbller provides visitors much more than amazing wines though. The winery's facilities include a beautiful tasting room and gift shop, which offers a wide array of wines, gourmet snacks, and wine-related gifts. The adjoining west wing invites visitors to enjoy a bottle of Röbller's finest in the beauty of a beamed ceiling, wood floors, and a fireplace. The atmosphere outside is just as delightful as it is inside. Röbller's outdoor pavilion and patio are excellent spots for a picnic, whether it is a full meal brought from home or an assortment of cheeses, crackers, and sausages purchased in the tasting room and gift shop. On weekends from October through May, live music entertains visitors on the patio, and the winery's annual Barbecue and Blues Festival and Reggae Sunsplash provide even more fun each summer for visitors young and old. Open year round, Röbller is a treat for any visitor on any day of the year.

ABOVE: A glass of Röbller wine will delight any wine lover.

ABOVE: Any visitor can find that perfect wine in Röbller's tasting room.

ABOVE: Röbller's Norton has won numerous state and national awards.

"A person with increasing knowledge and sensory education may derive infinite enjoyment from wine.

— Ernest Hemingway

Stone Hill Winery

Owners: Jim & Betty Held, Jon Held, Patty Held, & Thomas Held

Winemakers: Dave Johnson, Shaun Turnbull, & Tavis Harris

Region: Hermann

Established: 1847

Vineyard Acreage: 157 acres

Annual Production: 100,000 cases

Stone Hill Winery is perched prominently upon one of Hermann's picturesque hilltops, overlooking the town below. Each year, Stone Hill welcomes thousands of visitors who enjoy not only the award-winning wines and juices of this world-class winery, but also the region's Old-World charm and surrounding beauty.

Since its establishment in 1847, Stone Hill has undergone significant and inevitable changes. Early in its history, Stone Hill grew to be the second-largest winery in the United States. Its wines were world renowned, winning gold medals in eight World's Fairs, including Vienna in 1873 and Philadelphia in 1876. By the turn of the century, the winery was shipping 1,250,000 cases of wine each year. Unfortunately, the advent of Prohibition in 1920 killed the wine industry in Missouri, and Stone Hill's spectacular arched, underground cellars, the largest series of vaulted cellars in America, were converted into a mushroom-growing facility. In 1965 though, with their four small children in tow, owners Jim and Betty Held bought the winery and began the long process of restoring its charming buildings and underground cellars, which had fallen into disrepair after Prohibition.

Today, Stone Hill, which is listed on the National Register of Historic Places, is Missouri's oldest and most-awarded winery and one of Missouri's most-popular tourist attractions. With a breathtaking view of the town, the 13-acre complex contains a stately main building with its newly-remodeled gift shop, a modern production facility, the wonderful Vintage Restaurant, and 160-year-old underground cellars.

Stone Hill welcomes visitors with open arms and invites them to take a guided tour through its historic cavernous cellars and state-of-the-art production facility before settling in for a wine tasting in one of three elegant tasting rooms in the winery's main building. Additionally, in the same building where Stone Hill's original horse stable and carriage house were once located, visitors may now dine in casual comfort at the Vintage Restaurant, where German specialties are lovingly served along with steaks and other American dishes. Much care was taken in the 1979 restoration of the building to maintain as much of the original decor as possible. No visit to Stone Hill would be complete without browsing through the winery's spacious wine and gift shop. This magnificent showcase displays each of Stone Hill's many remarkable wines, along with countless wine-related items and souvenirs handsomely arranged throughout the 3,000-square-foot shop.

Regardless of the weather, Stone Hill's gracious hospitality awaits visitors every day of the year, though some days are more special than others. In addition to participating in the Hermann area's numerous popular festivals, Stone Hill hosts its own special events each year. In late August, the winery celebrates the beginning of the grape harvest with its Grape Stomp, a charity event that raises funds for Hermann's local Sheltered Workshop, and sponsors both the Cajun Concert in July and the Big Band Dance in August.

The only thing as impressive as Stone Hill's rich history and magnificent facilities is its wines. Keeping the family winemaking tradition alive, three of Jim and Betty's four children hold degrees in enology and viticulture. Stone Hill's winemaking team, which also includes senior winemaker David Johnson, winemaker Shaun Turnbull,

Stone Hill Winery

1110 Stone Hill Highway
Hermann, Missouri 65041
(800) 909-9463
www.stonehillwinery.com

Stone Hill's amazing underground cellars are the largest series of vaulted cellars in America.

and enologist Tavis Harris, produces wines that have been receiving international acclaim for years and have won more than 3,200 awards since 1993, which ranks Stone Hill among the nation's top award winners.

Using European-American hybrid grape varietals, including Chambourcin, Chardonel, Saint Vincent, Traminette, Vidal, and Vignoles, Stone Hill produces sophisticated wines that compare favorably to more popular varietals like Chardonnay and Merlot, and blends different varietals to produce its popular proprietary wines, which include the Golden Rhine, Hermannsberger, Rosé Montaigne, Steinberg Red, and Steinberg White. The winery also produces two amazing sparkling wines in its Blanc de Blancs and Brut Rosé. Saving the best for last though, according to many delighted visitors, Stone Hill is well known for its fine native-American varietals of Norton, Concord, and Pink Catawba. The Norton, Stone Hill's pride and joy, proves that Missouri can produce a big, full-bodied red wine of world-class stature.

Stone Hill's success has been as sweet as its Concord and as long lived and hardy as its Norton. The winery and its winemaking team have received such honors as Winemaker of the Year, Winegrower of the Year, Wine Growing Family of the Year, Missouri Small Business of the Year, and the Missouri Wine and Grape Board's Pioneer Award, and Stone Hill wines have won numerous Missouri Governor's Cup awards and thousands of other wine awards. The winery has achieved even greater national

ABOVE: In 1979, Stone Hill's former carriage house and horse barn was restored and made home to the winery's Vintage Restaurant.

RIGHT: The Vintage Restaurant caters to its visitors by serving traditional German cuisine, steaks and other American cuisine, and a full selection of Stone Hill's own award-winning wines.

prominence by being featured on *The Today Show* in 1994, in *Nations Business Weekly* in 1995, and on both *Discover America* and *The Early Show* in 2001. For Stone Hill, all of this recognition has been gratifying, but only incidental to its primary task: producing and marketing the finest wines and putting Hermann back on the map as a world-class wine-producing area.

ABOVE: *On a warm, sunny day, nothing compares to enjoying a bottle of Stone Hill wine and the spectacular view from the hillside overlooking the town of Hermann below.*

LEFT: *Stone Hill wines have won more than 3,200 awards since 1993, ranking the winery among the nation's top award winners.*

"*Winemaking is the combination of science, nature, and art to make something greater than the sum of its parts.*

— Tavis Harris, Stone Hill Winery enologist

Ozark Highlands Region

The Ozark Highlands region is an American Viticultural Area in south-central Missouri, spanning from just east of Jefferson City south as far as the Eleven Point River, which is considered by many to be the most pristine river in the Ozarks. The land in the region is drier than in other areas of the state, but the sandy-loam-and-clay composition of the soil allows it to retain moisture well. In fact, the Italian immigrants who first settled the region in the 1800s found this soil to be great for grape growing. While Prohibition temporarily caused a cease in wine production, the region's wine industry has slowly rebuilt itself while maintaining its Italian heritage, as evidenced in its many Italian-style wines.

In addition to excellent wines, the region offers visitors a wide array of leisure activities. The centerpiece of the region, the town of Saint James, is home to quite a collection of unique gift and antique shops, and visitors often enjoy making it a weekend trip by staying at a charming bed and breakfast. Nature lovers are also pleased to visit the region for its great selection of outdoor activities. Conveniently located just eight miles southeast of Saint James, Maramec Spring Park provides a wonderful escape. The Park is home to one of only four trout parks in Missouri, obviously providing for excellent trout fishing, and also has a nice reception center, a café, two museums, tennis courts, hiking trails, playgrounds, picnic areas, and a campground.

Just as importantly, because the region is so centrally located, it is easily accessible to visitors from anywhere in the state, allowing anyone to enjoy all that the Ozark Highlands region has to offer.

Ferrigno Vineyards & Winery

Region: Ozark Highlands
Established: 1982

Vineyard Acreage: 10 acres
Annual Production: 1,050 cases

As Fiorello LaGuardia, former mayor of New York City, once said, "I am certain that the good Lord never intended grapes to be made into grape jelly." Fortunately for Missouri wine lovers, Ferrigno Vineyards & Winery believed that grapes were never intended for just grape juice either.

Prior to the Ferrigno family's purchase in 1976, the previous owners of the property grew only Concord grapes. While some of the grapes were used by the owners to make homemade wines, primarily for consumption by their own family, most were sold to Welch's to be made into grape juice. Still, in large part due to the high quality of the grapes grown on the land, the small amount of homemade wines became both well known and well loved locally.

In 1976, the Ferrignos purchased the property and began planting European-American hybrid grapevines alongside the native-American Concord vines. For six long years, they

—87—

toiled in the vineyard and nurtured the young vines to ensure production of only the highest-quality grapes for their wines. Finally, in 1982, the winery opened its doors and welcomed visitors to enjoy its fine wines.

If spending an afternoon in the cool shade of a rustic wine garden overlooking the vineyard sounds appealing, then Ferrigno beckons. Visitors can sample each of the winery's 11 wonderful wines, as well as indulge in fine cheeses, Missouri sausages, and other snacks at the wine garden deli.

Ferrigno's wines are handcrafted using fresh grapes from its own vineyard which are then fermented, aged, and bottled on location in its production facility. The winery's dry and medium-dry wines are made in styles that complement a variety of foods, and its sweet wines are balanced to avoid an overly-sweet finish. Whether making its smooth and flavorful Seyval Blanc or its fruity and complex Chambourcin, all of Ferrigno's winemaking efforts are geared towards producing clean, flavorful wines of premium quality and distinctive character.

Ferrigno Vineyards & Winery

17301 State Route B
Saint James, Missouri 65559
(573) 265-7742

ABOVE: *Ferrigno's wine garden provides an intimate and comfortable outdoor setting for visitors to enjoy of a bottle of wine.*

WINE LIST

RED:
Chambourcin, Concord, Norton, Nouveau Red, Vino di Famiglia, & Viva Bacco Red

WHITE:
Primavera, Seyval Blanc, & Viva Bacco White

BLUSH:
Chambourcin Rosé & Viva Bacco Blush

If food is the body of good living, wine is its soul.

— Clifton Fadiman

Meramec Vineyards

Owner: Phyllis Meagher

Winemakers: Phyllis Meagher & Bob DeWitt

Region: Ozark Highlands

Established: 2000

Vineyard Acreage: 28 acres

Annual Production: 4,200 cases

Appropriately named, Meramec Vineyards sits in the small yet energetic community of Saint James, near the point where Meramec Spring flows into the Meramec River. The Spring is well known for its superb trout fishing, and the River is an important tributary of the Mississippi River, into which it flows just below the iconic Saint Louis Arch. The winery is a destination in its own right and is popular with visitors looking for fine wines and fun times.

Meramec has a rich history that began with Italians settling in the area in the early 20th century. The settlers brought their winemaking knowledge and skills from the Old World and began producing the same high-quality wines to which they were accustomed, though using new and interesting Missouri grape varietals. The Tessaro family first settled on the land, but it was the next owner who planted the first 15 acres of Concord grapevines.

Meramec was established in 1980 on the beautiful property with the original vineyard still growing. In the beginning, the grapes harvested in the vineyard were sold locally, and after time, they were used to make delicious fruit juices, some of which are still made and sold there today. Eventually though, Meramec expanded further into winemaking and officially opened as a winery in

January 2000.

Today, the winery produces 11 different wines, including five reds (Bistro Red, Classic Concord, New World Red, Norton, and Silvio's Red), four whites (Bistro Gold, Bistro White, New World White, and Vignoles), and two blushes (Catawba Blush and Sweet Cat). Winemakers Phyllis Meagher and Bob DeWitt take great pride in the high-quality wines they produce, which consistently take home medals from the Missouri Wine Competition. For younger visitors or those looking for something a little different, Meramec's three sparkling grape juices (Catawba, Concord, and Niagara) are wonderful choices.

Meramec's fine wines and juices are not the only things that make the winery unique: Meramec grows a rarely-found grape called the Stark's Star, which is a hybrid of the Catawba and Norton Grapes. Professor Joseph Bachman of Altus, Arkansas developed the Stark's Star in the late 1800s, but then sold the propagation rights to Stark Brothers Nurseries, which then introduced the grape at the Saint Louis World's Fair in 1904. The Stark's Star, which Meramec uses in its Silvio's Red, is known for its slight fruitiness and complex taste.

The winery offers visitors an attractive venue for the enjoyment of its wines. Its new processing-and-retail building is conveniently located just off Interstate 44 and features beautiful wooden beams and natural lighting. Delicious meals are available in the bistro, and the gift shop sells wines, foods, wine-related gifts, and other unique items, such as original artwork made by local artists. Meramec truly is the perfect place for any visitor to enjoy the fruit of the vine and the work of human hands.

Meramec Vineyards

600 State Route B
Saint James, Missouri 65559
(573) 265-7847
www.meramecvineyards.com

ABOVE: Each of Meramec's wonderful wines begins its life in the vineyard.

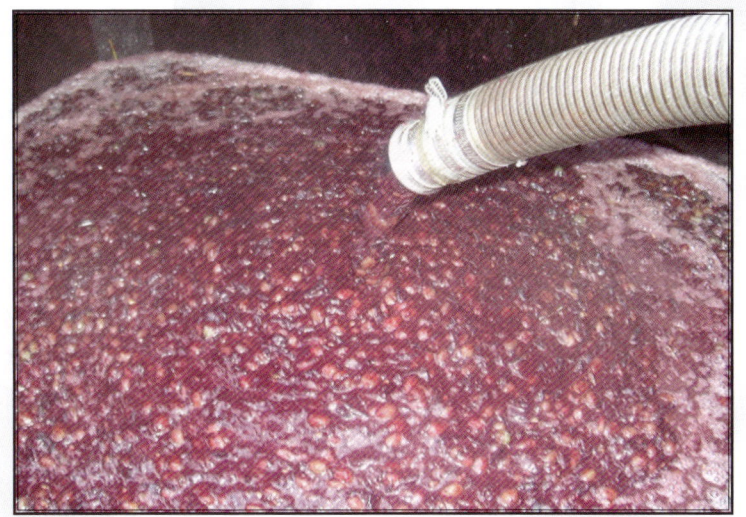

ABOVE: The winery takes care in each step of the winemaking process to ensure high-quality wines.

> *Wine is sunlight, held together by water.*
>
> — Galileo Galilei

Peaceful Bend Vineyard

Owners: Clyde Gill & Katherine Nott

Winemaker: Clyde Gill

Region: Ozark Highlands

Established: 1972

Just outside placid Steelville, along the quiet banks of the Meramec River, Peaceful Bend Vineyard delivers precisely what its name promises. From its picturesque, wooden cellar building, owners Clyde Gill and Katherine Nott serve Peaceful Bend's award-winning wines with friendly, personal service.

If visitors to Peaceful Bend feel like they have stepped back in time to the Old World, it is no surprise. The seeds of the winery were planted when Saint Louis-native Doctor Axel Arneson, the owner of the property nearly half a century ago, was on a trip to Europe. Arneson was so inspired by the French-estate wineries that he decided he had to have his own vineyard and winery upon returning to Missouri. Back home in 1965, he worked with his family to plant the property's first grapevines. Seven years later, after the vines were producing grapes and Arneson had learned the art of winemaking, the Arnesons opened a tasting room to share their wines with the world.

The Arneson family did not last as long on the property as the winery did. Peaceful Bend passed from owner to owner several times during the 1990s, but fortunately for wine lovers, Clyde and Katherine took ownership of the winery in spring 1998. Clyde learned winemaking through apprenticeship and study, and Katherine studied viticulture at Michigan State University. The blending of Clyde's winemaking skills and Katherine's viticulture knowledge was not the only perfect union at Peaceful Bend though. Under the winery's oak trees, the couple married in spring 1999.

Clyde and Katherine's expertise and passion have brought forth an array of wonderful wines. Peaceful Bend's Late Harvest Chardonel tops its list of sweet wines, which also contains such treats as its Hussah Valley Rosé and

Sweet River White. For visitors preferring drier wines, the winery produces Forché Renault and Meramec, both reds, and its Chardonel, a lovely barrel-fermented white, among others. Many of Peaceful Bend's wines are named for rivers and creeks flowing near the winery.

It is impossible to avoid relaxation in the seclusion of the winery's 72-acre, wooded estate. Visitors may take a stroll in the wine garden, wind their way down a path to the Meramec River's bank, or simply sit back and enjoy a bottle of Peaceful Bend wine in the shade of the age-old oak trees. Visitors who just cannot pull themselves away at the end of a perfect day at the winery do not have to. A lovely two-bedroom cottage is located on the property, complete with a stocked kitchen and bottle of Peaceful Bend wine for visitors to enjoy. The rustic yet comfortable accommodations offer visitors the opportunity to truly enjoy the full Peaceful Bend experience.

Peaceful Bend Vineyard

1942 Highway T
Steelville, Missouri 65565
(573) 775-3000
www.peacefulbend.com

LEFT: Peaceful Bend is the perfect retreat from the fast pace of life.

BELOW: No matter the season or weather, Peaceful Bend definitely lives up to its name.

BELOW: The air at the winery is always filled with sounds of laughter.

" *Where there is no wine, there is no love.*

— Euripides

Saint James Winery

Owner: Patricia Hofherr

Winemaker: Andrew Meggitt

Region: Ozark Highlands

Established: 1970

Vineyard Acreage: 300 acres

Annual Production: 200,000 cases

The Ozark Highlands region, fondly referred to as the "Little Italy of the Ozarks" because of the Italian immigrants who first settled the area more than a century ago, is home to some of the most-successful and finest wineries in Missouri. One of the most well known is Saint James Winery. Established by James and Patricia Hofherr in 1970, Saint James has become a cornerstone of the Missouri wine industry and one of the most-respected and often-awarded wineries throughout the entire United States. Today, owner Patricia Hofherr and winemaker Andrew Meggitt, take great pride in continuing Saint James' fine tradition of producing high-quality, award-winning wines to be enjoyed by wine lovers from coast to coast, but especially those in its home state of Missouri.

The entire Hofherr family has worked hard over the years to build a reputation for excellent wines with a uniquely Midwest flavor. From the day Saint James opened its doors in 1970, running the winery has been a family affair. The Hofherrs, children and all, tended the grapevines and handpicked the grapes in the winery's vineyard for Saint James' first vintage of wines: 3,500 cases of its Velvet Red and Velvet White. Although the Hofherr children have grown up since the winery produced its first bottles, they remain a vital part of Saint James' current success. In fact, Andrew Hofherr serves as the winery's Chief Operations Officer, while Peter Hofherr serves as its Chief Financial Officer.

Both children are obviously well educated in winemaking. Andrew studied viticulture at the University of Arkansas and is considered a leading authority on the subject throughout the Midwest, frequently speaking on the topic. Peter has a degree in microbiology from Auburn University and an M.B.A. from Georgia State University. He was also previously employed by the Missouri Department of Agriculture, where he served for two years as its director.

Winemaker Andrew Meggitt is another key part of Saint James' success. A native of New Zealand, Meggitt has been in the wine industry since 1990. He holds a bachelor's degree from the University of Canterbury and a postgraduate degree in viticulture and enology from Lincoln University. Meggitt's winemaking enthusiasm and skill, combined with Saint James' use of state-of-the-art winemaking equipment and techniques, allow Saint James wines to capture all of the flavors created in the vineyards, resulting in true, flavorful wines that have delighted visitors for decades and made the

Saint James Winery

540 Sidney Street
Saint James, Missouri 65559
(573) 265-7912
www.stjameswinery.com

LEFT: Winemaker Andrew Meggitt takes great pride in the high quality of Saint James' award-winning wines.

RIGHT: Saint James' vineyards produce the perfect grapes for its big and fruity wines.

winery one of the most-awarded in the nation.

According to American Gold Medal Wines, a guide that tracks the gold medals awarded in top regional, national, and international wine competitions each year, Saint James ranked fourth among all American wineries for gold medals won in 2007 domestic wine competitions. In total, the winery took home a total of 424 medals in 2007, including 23 double golds, 62 golds, 175 silvers, and 164 bronzes. Saint James was also awarded a platinum medal at the prestigious Critics Challenge International Wine Competition for its 2005 Chardonel Port. This is nothing new for the winery though, because it has won thousands of state and national awards over the years.

Saint James produces more than 30 different wines from the Catawba, Chardonel, Concord, Norton, Seyval, and Vignoles grapes grown in its vineyards. While there is an amazing variety of wines on Saint James' wine list, ranging from dry reds to sweet dessert and fruit wines, one thing is

ABOVE: Saint James' history is as deep and as rich as its award-winning wines.

BELOW: The winery goes to great measures to ensure wines of the highest quality.

BELOW: Visitors can find almost any wine-related item in Saint James' gift shop.

— 95 —

consistent across all of its wines: top-notch quality. Not surprisingly, the wonderful quality and great selection of its wines have not gone unnoticed by wine lovers. In fact, Saint James wines are so widely acclaimed and well loved that they are available in 14 different states across the country.

Still, visitors continue to flock to the winery from near and far to experience all that Saint James has to offer. To better accommodate these visitors, the winery expanded its cellar and warehouse and renovated its combined tasting room and gift pavilion by adding custom ceramic tiling and stunning woodwork. With over 10,000 square feet of space now, visitors have plenty of room to enjoy each Saint James wine at the winery's complimentary, self-serve tasting bar or to browse the gift pavilion's gourmet foods, stemware, gift baskets, and unique wine accessories. Saint James also offers a convenient schedule of free public tours on the weekends, and accommodates requests for tours during the week. Stepping outside the wheelchair-accessible facility, visitors also find an outdoor picnic area beneath a beautiful grape arbor.

Although Saint James is one of the most-awarded wineries in the United States, visitors do not need to see the awards to know of the winery's success in quality winemaking. Rather, they can just pour themselves a glass, as Saint James wines speak for themselves.

LEFT: With vineyards totaling 300 acres, the winery is sure to have enough wine for every visitor.

BELOW: Saint James is able to accommodate and happily welcomes groups of all sizes.

"*Wine can be considered with good reason as the most healthful and hygienic of all beverages.*

— Louis Pasteur

Ozark Mountain Region

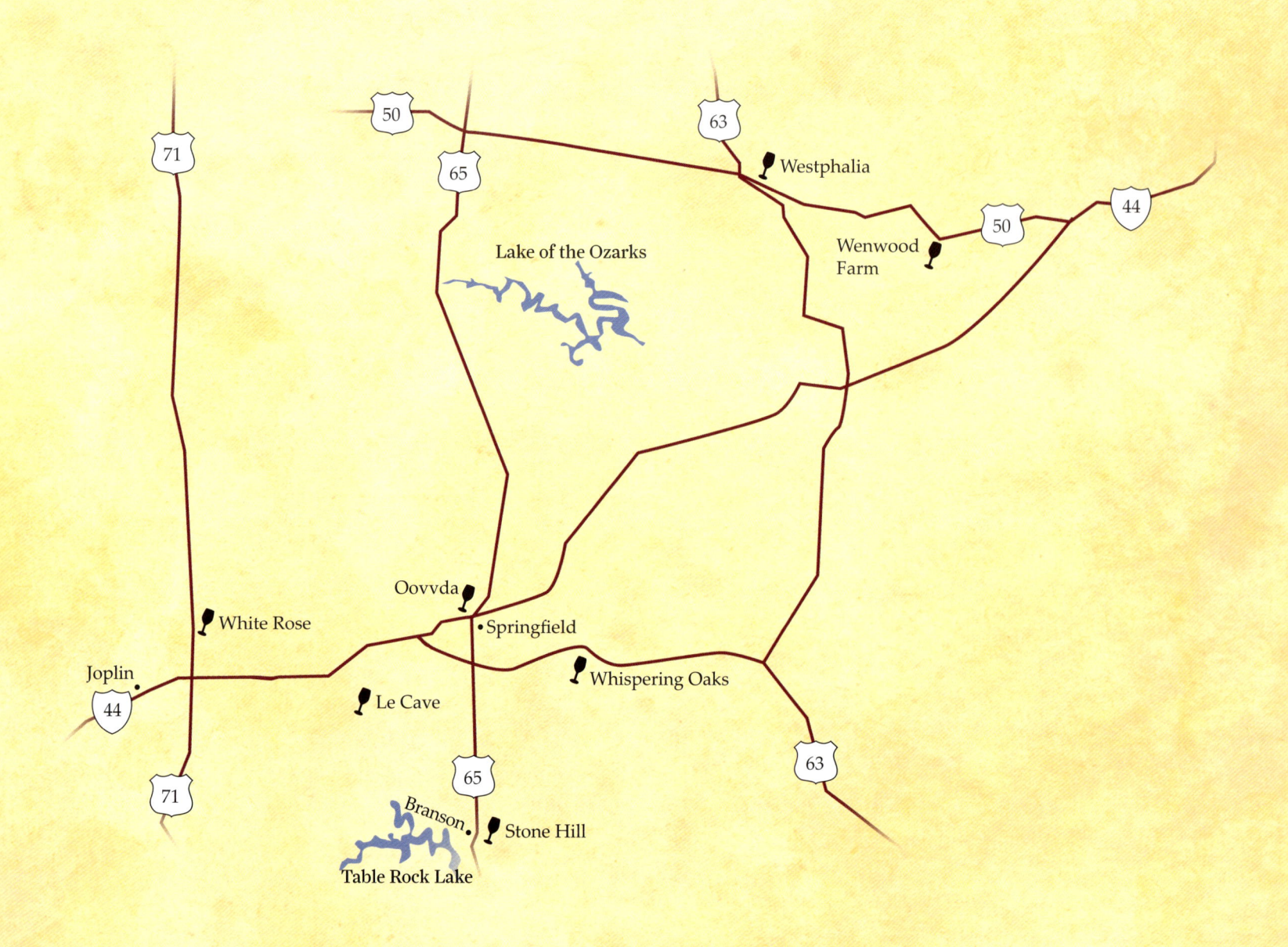

Wineries located in southern Missouri are proudly part of the sixth-largest American Viticultural Area in the United States: the Ozark Mountain region. Covering 3,520,000 acres, the region encompasses most of the southern half of Missouri as well as portions of northern Arkansas and Oklahoma. Being so large, five smaller American Viticultural Areas have actually been established within its borders to recognize those smaller regions whose climate, soil, or other growing conditions create unique areas for viticulture. The region's wineries are quickly making their mark on the state's wine industry. At Stone Hill Winery in Branson, for example, nearly half a million visitors stop by each year to sample wines, tour the winery, and get a taste of Stone Hill while vacationing in the southern part of the state.

Located within the region are the state's third-largest city of Springfield, the popular tourist destination of Branson, and the historic town of Carthage. Springfield's world-famous Bass Pro Shops offers visitors the opportunity to explore its Outdoor World Fish and Wildlife Museum, purchase a wide variety of sports equipment and outdoor recreation items, and dine in style at its Hemingway's Blue Water Café. Less than an hour south of Springfield is Branson, home to beautiful Table Rock Lake, countless world-renowned shows and other attractions for all ages, championship golf courses, and very fine overnight accommodations. Only an hour southwest of Springfield, in Carthage, visitors can enjoy the historic mansions lined with the same Carthage marble that fronts both the Missouri and the United States Capitol buildings, or stop by the delightful Precious Moments Park and Chapel. No matter where in the Ozark Mountain region visitors find themselves, fine wines and world-class attractions await.

Le Cave Vineyards

Le Cave Vineyards

6696 Jasmine Road
Billings, Missouri 65610
(417) 744-4122
www.lecavevineyards.com

Owners: Larry & Beth White
Winemaker: Larry White
Region: Ozark Mountain
Established: 2004
Vineyard Acreage: 16 acres
Annual Production: 700 cases

Larry and Beth White, owners of Le Cave Vineyards, truly understand the key to keeping visitors happy: a location away from the fast pace of the city, a relaxing atmosphere, down-home hospitality, and of course, a great selection of wonderful wines. After being greeted by the canine welcoming committee and shouts from the outdoor tasting deck, visitors cannot help but uncork a bottle of Le Cave wine and toss their worries to the wind. The winery's "no standing" rule ensures that feet are kicked up, wineglasses are tipped back, and laughter fills the air.

Le Cave is located on a historic farm in the Ozark Mountain region, about 25 miles southwest of Springfield. The Whites have gone to great lengths to maintain the original feel of the farm that the winery now occupies. The old dairy barn on the property was renovated to accommodate Le Cave's visitors, complete with an indoor tasting loft and an outdoor tasting deck in the shade of beautiful walnut trees. The wire-brushed, clear-span bent-wood ceiling, widescreen television, and fireplace provide the finishing touches to make Le Cave an ideal retreat.

Le Cave produces a dozen fine wines, most-notably including its Chambourcin dessert wine, Frontenac,

ABOVE: Le Cave's tasting room is the perfect place to sample great wines before picking up a souvenir in the winery's gift shop.

and Vignoles, and plans to continue adding new wines to its already-impressive list. In producing its wines, Le Cave operates on the simple yet essential principle that producing the finest wines requires the finest fruits. Le Cave prides itself on growing and harvesting its own grapes and handcrafting its own high-quality wines.

Le Cave's family atmosphere is what sets it apart from other wineries. The winery is family owned, and the entire White family, from Larry and Beth all the way down to their grandchildren, helps bring Le Cave wines from the grapevine to the lips of wine lovers throughout the state. The atmosphere at the winery even has visitors feeling like a part of the family. While Le Cave hosts such fun events as horseshoe tournaments and pig roasts, even less eventful days are loved by visitors. The winery offers cheeses, chocolates, and brunch baskets to complement its wines, and provides fun, live music to delight its picnickers.

With such a strong dedication to producing quality wines and satisfying visitors, Le Cave's future looks very bright. Although the winery's popularity is sure to grow, Le Cave's visitors will always find great wines served by friendly folks in a delightful and relaxing atmosphere.

ABOVE: Despite advances in technology, the winemaking process still requires the careful attention of a skilled winemaker.

BELOW: Le Cave is a family-owned winery with a down-home, country feel.

" *Wine is inspiring and adds greatly to the joy of living.*

— Napoleon Bonaparte

Oovvda Winery

Owners: Brian & Fran Overboe, Damon Overboe, & Nathan Overboe

Winemaker: Brian Overboe

Region: Ozark Mountain

Established: 2005

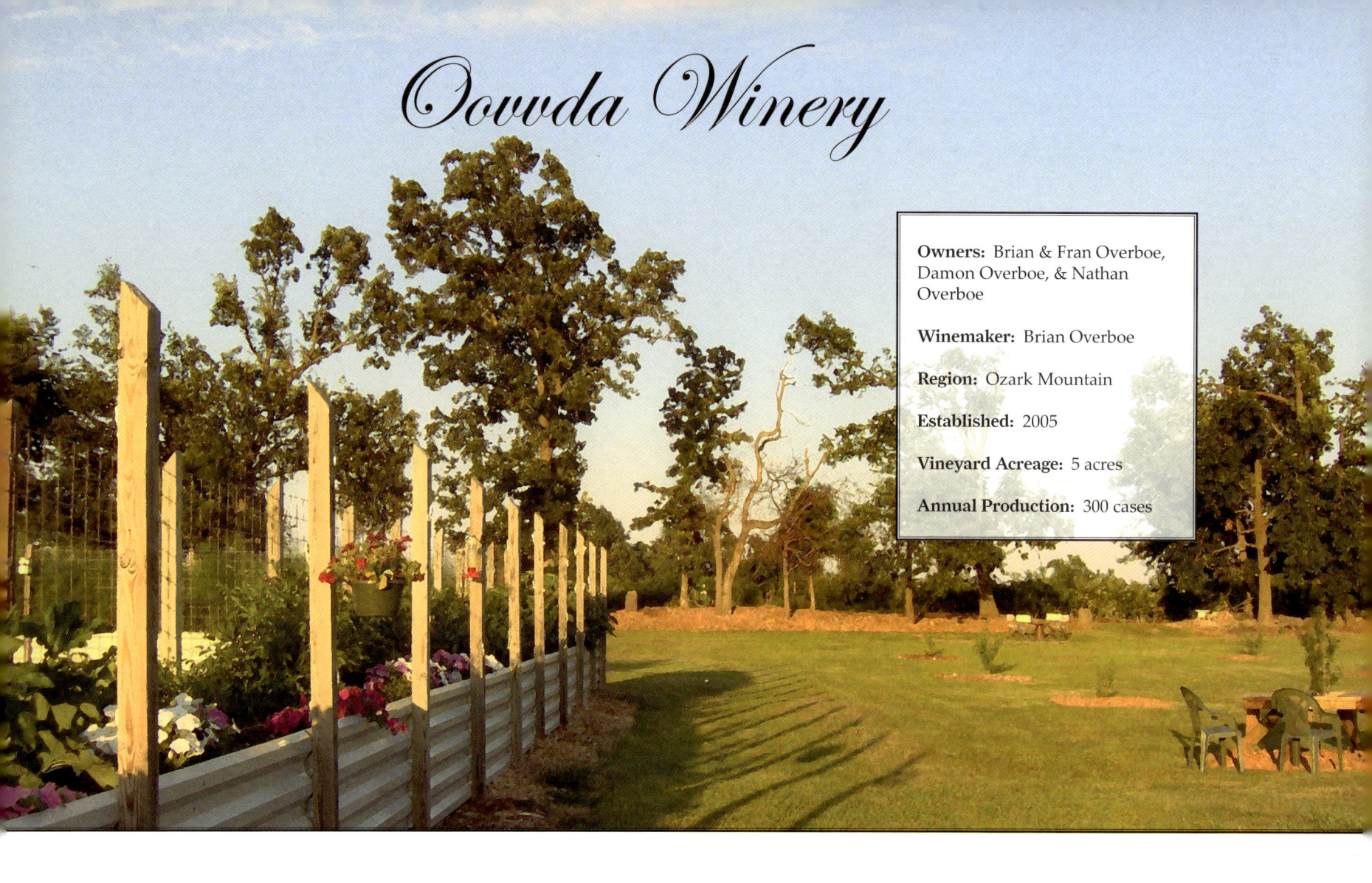

Vineyard Acreage: 5 acres

Annual Production: 300 cases

In the heart of the Ozarks, just north of Springfield, lies Oovvda Winery, a small, family-owned winery offering a splendid assortment of fresh fruit wines. Members of the Overboe family, who have been making wines for generations, refer to themselves as "Viking Vintners," because their family tree can be traced back to 1192 A.D. in Norway.

Oovvda, established in 2005, takes pride in producing wines made from only the finest fruits, including estate-grown red raspberries, black raspberries, and cherries. Each of Oovvda's wines is handcrafted to bring out the natural flavors of the fruit, and the search is constantly on to introduce new and intriguing wines to its wine list.

Because the wine list is both extensive and impressive, visitors often find it difficult to find just one favorite wine. Still, several wines have proven consistently popular among Oovvda's visitors, including its Black Raspberry, Blackberry, Blueberry, Cherry Tart Pie, Concord, Red Raspberry, and Strawberry. Depending on the season, less common types of wines are available as well. All Oovvda wines are available in dry, semi-dry, semi-sweet, and sweet versions, so as to appeal to the taste of any visitor, and can be sampled in the winery's elegant tasting room.

As a general rule, Oovvda recommends that visitors let their own tastes prevail. Because wines can always be sweetened, but cannot be made drier, Oovvda suggests ordering drier wines before sweeter wines. Visitors seem to agree, as most actually prefer the drier wines, which are naturally complemented by the sweet finish of the fruits used in their production.

Even with so many wonderful options, the true selection is even wider, as Oovvda offers custom finishing of any wine in its already-expansive selection. This distinctive service allows a visitor to select any of Oovvda's wines, have the wine adjusted to the sweetness level that best suits the visitor's taste, and watch his or her custom wine be bottled. The finishing touch is a personalized label, which can commemorate a special event, make a unique gift, or just provide a wonderful Oovvda keepsake. Because of the time and work that goes into producing these customized wines, they are shipped directly to customers at home once the extensive process is complete.

The knowledgeable staff at the winery enjoys helping those visitors who are not quite connoisseurs. From proper storage and serving suggestions to wine recommendations based on personal preferences, Oovvda is dedicated to helping each visitor enjoy every aspect of his or her experience.

No experience would be complete without taking time to relax in Oovvda's beautiful outdoor wine garden. Featuring a fire pit, mellow music, hummingbirds, and lawn games, the atmosphere in the wine garden is always fun yet still relaxing. Visitors are encouraged to bring a picnic basket or even just snacks to complement their wines. Oovvda, like its wine garden, is the perfect escape for friends and family of all ages.

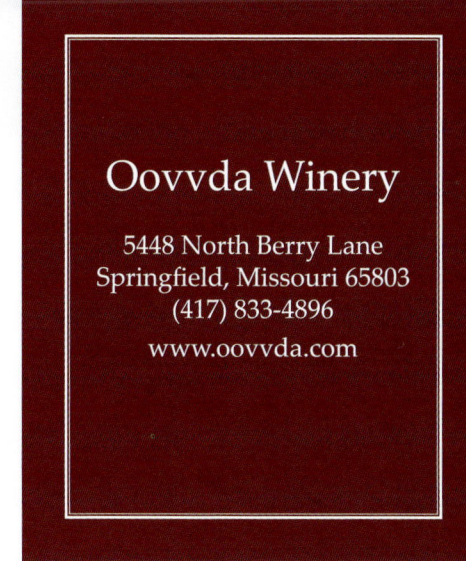

Oovvda Winery

5448 North Berry Lane
Springfield, Missouri 65803
(417) 833-4896
www.oovvda.com

LEFT: *Every visitor is treated like royalty, especially in the luxurious tasting room.*

BELOW: *Oovvda's wine garden provides an atmosphere of both fun and relaxation.*

"*When there is plenty of wine, sorrow and worry take wing.*

— Ovid

Stone Hill Winery

Owners: Jim & Betty Held, Jon Held, Patty Held, & Thomas Held

Winemakers: Dave Johnson, Shaun Turnbull, & Tavis Harris

Region: Ozark Mountain

Established: 1986

Annual Production: 6,000 cases

Visitors to Branson may be surprised to find that Missouri's oldest and most-awarded winery is also one of the town's most-popular attractions. With 12,000 square feet of space, Stone Hill Winery's Branson location has been entertaining visitors since 1986. The winery, located at the junction of Highway 165 and Green Mountain Drive (just two blocks south of world-famous 76 Country Music Boulevard), delights thousands of visitors daily with a free, fun-filled tour and an unforgettable tasting of Stone Hill's many award-winning wines and juices.

Upon arrival at Stone Hill, most visitors start their adventure with one of the winery's hour-long, guided tours, which begin every 15 minutes. Fun, humorous, and educational, the tour guides visitors through the huge winery complex, where they witness the step-by-step winemaking process. The tour begins with the presentation of a short film, which depicts the proud tradition of Missouri winemaking and highlights the vineyards and cellars of Stone Hill's impressive Hermann location. Next, visitors are invited to take in the delightful aromas of the winery's maturing Sherry, which is first baked and then aged in oak barrels. Visitors then get to watch the actual bottling of Stone Hill's famous Spumante.

The tour ends in one of the winery's six tasting rooms, where visitors can sample their way through an array of Stone Hill's award-winning wines and juices. Of course, if time is of the essence, visitors are welcome to skip the tour and head straight to a tasting room. The wines range from the dry, full-bodied Norton, a red wine that has captured international recognition, to the sweet, fruity Pink Catawba. With Stone Hill's amazing wine selection and quality, each visitor is sure to find that perfect wine within the wide spectrum of red, white, blush, spumante, and dessert wines available.

Stone Hill's Cream Sherry, in particular, is not to be forgotten, and is a unique, intriguing, and delicious addition to the winery's lineup. Stone Hill began its Sherry production in 1993 and bottled its first vintage in July 1999. Unlike wine production, the philosophy behind Sherry production is to subject the Sherry to increased temperatures and increased contact with air. Stone Hill's winemakers carefully select a sweetened wine and fortify it with a clear grape brandy. The fortified wine is then baked in jacketed, stainless-steel tanks for three to four

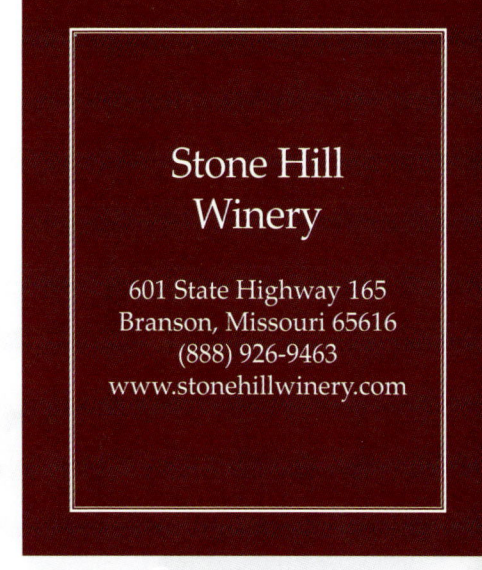

Stone Hill Winery

601 State Highway 165
Branson, Missouri 65616
(888) 926-9463
www.stonehillwinery.com

LEFT: Visitors love leaving Stone Hill with wines and other gifts.

months at temperatures near 130 degrees Fahrenheit. The jackets are circulated with hot water to cause the baking process. While the fortified wine is baking, it is aerated with oxygen. Combined with the heating process and the fortified wine's relatively-high sugar content, this aeration gives the Sherry its typical caramel flavor and color. After the baking process is complete, the Sherry is barreled to age for three to five years. During the aging process, the Sherry continues to darken in color and develops a rich, nutty flavor that becomes more and more complex with time. This barrel aging is what gives the Sherry its

ABOVE: Stone Hill wines range from the dry, full-bodied Norton, a red wine that has captured international recognition, to the sweet and fruity Pink Catawba and Concord.

BELOW: Most visitors start their adventure by taking the winery's fun, humorous, and educational guided tour.

amazing character. After careful monitoring for perfect flavor, Stone Hill's winemakers end the aging process and bottle the winery's Cream Sherry for enjoyment by all.

The adventure does not end with a tasting of Stone Hill's spectacular wines. Visitors are invited to browse the winery's large selection of quality wine-related items in the gift shop. With such a variety, there is sure to be something for each and every visitor to take home as a souvenir or a gift for a loved one.

As visitors quickly discover, Stone Hill prides itself on capturing and invigorating each of the five senses. Sight: The tour offers visitors the opportunity to view a short video about the winemaking tradition at Stone Hill and a Spumante-bottling demonstration. Smell: The air is always filled with the rich caramel and hazelnut aromas created during the baking process of the winery's Cream Sherry. Sound: Laughter can be heard each day throughout the winery, creating a fun and exciting atmosphere. Taste: It does not get any better than at Stone Hill, where visitors can taste the winery's array of dry, semi-dry, sweet, fortified, and sparkling wines and grape juices. Touch: No visit would be complete without picking up a book, shirt, bottle of Stone Hill wine, or any other item from the gift shop.

Branson is all about entertainment, and Stone Hill is no exception. Visitors expect to be entertained, and Stone Hill goes out of its way to exceed every expectation by providing an interesting, educational, and most of all, fun experience for all.

TOUR INFORMATION

COST: Free! One of the only free tours in Branson.

AGES: All ages, young and old.

LENGTH: Typically one hour, but tours can be adjusted to fit groups' schedules.

SCHEDULE: Every 15 minutes.

GROUPS: Walk-up groups are accomodated as the schedule permits.

ACCESSIBILITY: All one level and wheelchair accessible.

FEATURES: Tour of the Cream Sherry production facility, demonstration of the Spumante bottling process, tasting of award-winning wines and juices, and more!

For a cup is in the hand of the Lord, and the wine foams.

— Psalms 75:8

Wenwood Farm Winery

Owners: Tom Kalb & Laura Neese
Winemaker: Tom Kalb
Region: Ozark Mountain
Established: 2001
Annual Production: 1,700 cases

Wenwood Farm Winery
1132 Brick Church Road
Bland, Missouri 65014
(573) 437-3443
www.wenwoodfarmwinery.com

Situated in the foothills of beautiful central Missouri, Wenwood Farm Winery combines classy wine with country charm. While the winery has only been open since 2001, the property has a much longer history. For generations, award-winning Guernsey cattle were raised on the family dairy farm that occupied the land. When the husband and wife team of Tom Kalb and Laura Neese took over management, as fourth-generation owners of the family farm, they decided to phase out milk production and phase in another time-honored, Missouri tradition: winemaking.

Wenwood Farm's transition from a dairy farm to a winery was not unexpected. Tom had spent much of his life in the wine industry. At the young age of 14, he worked as a tank scrubber and stock boy at a Wollersheim Winery, a small winery in his Wisconsin hometown. As Tom gained experience, he rose through the ranks of the winery and eventually became its general manager and head winemaker. In 1996, Tom moved from Wisconsin to Missouri and worked for a few years at Stone Hill Winery in Hermann. With decades of experience, Tom and Laura set off on their own and opened Wenwood Farm in 2001.

As a result of his many experiences, including working under a French winemaker at Wollersheim, Tom prefers to produce wines using a European winemaking style. That is, he prefers to blend the best grape varietals available into each wine, rather than merely producing single-varietal wines. Because Wenwood Farm's European-style winemaking is more easily supported by purchasing grapes from a variety of different growers than by harvesting grapes from a single vineyard, the winery does not have its own vineyard. Still, Wenwood Farm plans to plant several acres of grapevines in the coming years to be able to make estate-bottled wines.

Each of Wenwood Farm's wines is unique and special, some having even been infused with the juices of different fruits, such as cranberries or cherries. Wenwood Farm produces a full-bodied, dry red; a light-bodied, dry red; a refreshingly crisp, dry white with citrus tones and a lingering finish; a semi-dry white with a cranberry infusion; a semi-sweet white with a cherry infusion, which gives the wine a refreshing and fruity kick; a sweet, spatlese-style wine with a slightly tart finish; a sweet blush with a hint of strawberry; a sweet red; a luscious dessert wine; a Port-style wine; and various seasonal offerings.

Whichever Wenwood Farm wines visitors choose to sample, they quickly find the winery to be an excellent venue for relaxation and wine tasting. It has ample space to accommodate large groups, but it is intimate enough for a weekend picnic with family or friends, and its gift shop has something for every visitor. Throughout the year, the winery offers live entertainment under its rustic pavilion. It has spring, summer, and autumn festivals, Saturday-evening music in the summer, and afternoon music in the spring and fall. The winery also has various events throughout the winter. No matter the season, Wenwood Farm has plenty of wonderful times and fine wines for visitors to enjoy.

ABOVE: Wenwood Farm is all about friends, family, and fantastic wines.

BELOW: Wenwood Farm's various festivals are held year round, ensuring that the great fun and great wines it provides are available to visitors anytime.

Men are like wine - some turn to vinegar, but the best improve with age.

— Pope John XXIII

Westphalia Vineyards

Westphalia Vineyards

182 Brewery Lane
Westphalia, Missouri 65085
(573) 455-2950
www.westphaliavineyards.com

Owners: Terry & Mary Neuner
Winemaker: Terry Neuner
Region: Ozark Mountain
Established: 2005
Vineyard Acreage: 10 acres
Annual Production: 5,000 cases

The beautiful town of Westphalia, the "Pearl of Osage County," is located in central Missouri where the tranquil Maries River ribbons past limestone bluffs, lush farmland, and picturesque vineyards. In the 1830s, a group of German artisans and farmers settled in this fertile, tree-covered area, because it resembled their beloved home province of Westfalen. These hard-working and self-sufficient people brought to the New World their faith, strong traditions, and good humor. They also brought with them some of the finer things in life, including their love for and skill in winemaking.

In 2005, the Neuner family established Westphalia Vineyards, continuing the winemaking traditions of their German ancestors. In 1991, years before the Neuners began making wines, they purchased a 400-acre farm in the Maries River Valley near Westphalia. Tenants had used the land for many years to grow barley, corn, and milo and as fresh pasture for grazing cattle herds. Sadly, the majestic stone farmhouse, built by the wealthy, German-immigrant Porth family in the 1840s, had not been used as a residence for almost a century and had fallen into disrepair.

Today, Westphalia's wine production takes place just down a gravel road from the crumbling ruins of the Porths' 1840s brewery. The production facility is located in an immaculately-refurbished barn that was built during the same era as the brewery. Once filled with carriages and other horse-drawn farm equipment, the barn is now modern, sanitary, and perfect for winemaking.

Westphalia's handcrafted wines also owe their quality to their maker. Before establishing the winery, owner and winemaker Terry Neuner earned a master's degree in biochemistry from the University of Missouri-Columbia and worked for several years as a research chemist for the Missouri Farmer's Association. Not coincidentally,

Terry's expertise at MFA was in fermentation, where he was a pioneer in ethanol uses for fuel. Terry brings his full science background, agricultural skills, and fermentation knowledge to fruition in the wines he produces. He uses natural, time-honored processes to make Westphalia's award-winning wines.

Westphalia wines have won recognition in national competitions, and the town's residents take pride in their prizewinning local winery. In the inaugural National Norton Wine Festival competition, the winery's 2006 Norton Reserve was awarded a gold medal, one of only six gold medals awarded among the 113 wines entered. Westphalia adds no sulfites during its production process and exclusively uses Missouri-white-oak barrels for aging, creating fresh and vigorous wines.

Westphalia's production barn and vineyard are open only for pre-arranged, private tours. This allows the winery to focus on wine production rather than on tasting-room maintenance. Owners Terry and Mary Neuner established the winery in hopes of bringing people together. Their sons, Eric Neuner and Paul Neuner, along with family friend Tim Pingelton, assist in the vineyard. Pingelton worked for four years at Boulevard Brewing Company in Kansas City and has transferred his expertise in filtration and fermentation science to winemaking at Westphalia. Additionally, friends often stop by to help out with pruning or bottling or just to enjoy wonderful wines in a delightful atmosphere. After a long day of crushing grapes or cleaning barrels, the Neuners enjoy nothing more than relaxing on the back deck of the barn overlooking the vineyard while sharing a bottle of Westphalia's finest with family and friends.

ABOVE: Westphalia wines pair delightfully with many different foods.

BELOW: The view of the winery's vineyard is both stunning and relaxing.

"*There is nothing like wine for conjuring up feelings of contentment and goodwill. It is less of a drink than an experience, an evocation, a spirit. It produces sensations that defy description.*

— Thomas Conklin

Whispering Oaks Vineyard & Winery

Owners: Larry & Miriam Green

Winemaker: Larry Green

Region: Ozark Mountain

Established: 1997

Vineyard Acreage: 13 acres

Annual Production: 600 cases

Whispering Oaks Vineyard & Winery is a lovely winery offering visitors peace and quiet amidst nature's beauty for their wine-tasting enjoyment. The winery, which takes its name from the beautiful oak forests of the area, is located in the beautiful Gasconade River watershed in southwest Missouri. With its vineyard overlooking a picturesque valley just north of the second-highest point in the state, Whispering Oaks is simply one of nature's finest gifts to the wine industry.

Owners Larry and Miriam Green have owned the property since 1968. Nearly three decades later, in 1997, they made the decision to plant a vineyard and establish a winery. After another decade of lovingly tending the grapevines and beginning to produce wines from their grapes, Whispering Oaks has become quite an impressive winery. The wines produced at this family-owned winery showcase the distinctive flavors imparted by the rocky Ozark Highlands soil into its grapes. While Whispering Oaks wines have been delighting visitors for years, Larry, who is also the winery's winemaker, maintains a consistent goal: to produce wines superior to the previous year's wines.

Whispering Oaks produces nine wonderful wines, from light, fruity wines to full-bodied, complex wines, to meet the different tastes of its many visitors. From the skilled hands of its winemaker come the Catawba, Norton, Saint Vincent, semi-dry Vidal Blanc, semi-sweet Vidal Blanc, Vignoles, Whispering Oaks Red, Whispering Oaks Rosé, and Whispering Oaks White.

After sampling each of these fine Whispering Oaks wines in the winery's tasting room, visitors can retire to the picnic deck with a bottle of their favorite wine to enjoy the wonderful view of the Ozarks countryside. Visitors can also prearrange a tour of the well-manicured vineyard, where each bottle of Whispering Oaks wine is born. Each grapevine in the vineyard is given undivided attention to ensure high-quality grapes. By maintaining this same attention to detail and high quality throughout the grape-growing and winemaking processes, from the tending of the grapevines to the corking of the bottles, Whispering Oaks ensures that each bottle will contain the finest wine possible.

Aside from fine wines and natural beauty, Whispering Oaks provides visitors a unique and fun opportunity to share in the winemaking process.

Whispering Oaks Vineyard & Winery

520 Lucky Road
Seymour, Missouri 65746
(417) 935-4103
www.whisperingoakswinery.com

LEFT: From the winery's wooden porch, visitors can take in the view with a glass of wine in hand.

RIGHT: Whispering Oaks' tasting room provides a shady retreat on a hot summer day.

The spirit of wine sang in my glass, and I listened with love to his sonorous music, his flushed and magnificent song.

— William Ernest Henley

White Rose Winery

Owners: Jim & Jan O'Haro
Winemaker: Jim O'Haro
Region: Ozark Mountain

Established: 1998
Vineyard Acreage: 10 acres
Annual Production: 1,500 cases

White Rose Winery takes visitors on a unique trip back in time to a dairy farm located on the estate of a wealthy businessman. Today, many of the property's original structures still stand and have been carefully renovated to provide visitors modern comforts while maintaining their century-old charm.

White Rose invites visitors to enjoy a glass of wine at the tasting bar in its Carthage-marble mansion, which sits amidst a pristine 10-acre vineyard. In addition to the historic mansion, the property's original carriage house, which currently houses the winery's winemaking facility, sits proudly at the rear of the property near the vineyard. Not all of the winemaking process takes place in the former carriage house though. White Rose wines are actually aged in the cellar of the mansion, which also served as the home's original wine cellar.

Despite White Rose's reputation for making great wines, owners Jim and Jan O'Haro had no intention of making wines, let alone operating a winery, when they purchased the property. Instead, they just wanted a beautiful place to call home. Eventually though, friends and family convinced the O'Haros to share the mansion's beauty with others, and White Rose was born. The idea of a winery came as no surprise to those who knew the O'Haros well though. For more than 40 years, Jim had been perfecting the art of winemaking, information that he loves sharing with visitors.

The grapes that go into each of White Rose's wonderful wines are hand picked in the winery's vineyard. The winery produces a wide range of wines, including Cabernet Franc, Cayuga White, Chardonel, Claret, Lady in Red, Lady in White, Marechal Foch, Norton, Saint Vincent, Saint Vincent Nouveau, Spring River Red, Spring River White, Strawberry, and Sweet Lady in Red. Each of these wines can be tasted at the winery's tasting bar.

White Rose has much more to offer visitors than just wonderful wines. The winery also serves up delicious foods in its charming restaurant. The O'Haros stay true to their Irish heritage by offering visitors the best of traditional Irish cuisine, as well as a variety of customary American entrees. By reservation, the mansion's beautifully-decorated dining room will host dinner parties up to 12 for a truly-unforgettable dining experience, and for special occasions or events, visitors can even reserve the entire mansion.

For those looking for an overnight retreat, White Rose provides delightful accommodations in its bed and breakfast. Visitors are treated to an afternoon tea and, of course, a full, formal Irish breakfast. The rare historic comfort provided by White Rose is well worth the visit, and many overnight visitors find themselves returning again and again.

Whether visitors are searching for a great selection of fine wines, a delicious hand-prepared dinner, or a weekend retreat in historic comfort, a visit to White Rose should not be missed.

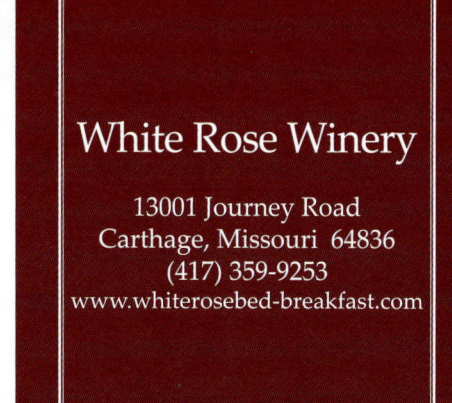

White Rose Winery

13001 Journey Road
Carthage, Missouri 64836
(417) 359-9253
www.whiterosebed-breakfast.com

ABOVE: Visitors can enjoy a bottle of White Rose wine in the ambiance of a beautiful, age-old mansion.

RIGHT: White Rose's tasting room bar is located in the mansion's historic gathering room.

" *Winemaking is both an art and a science. You can make great wine with art alone, but to repeatedly make great wine requires science.*

— *Jim O'Haro, White Rose Winery owner and winemaker*

Southeast Region

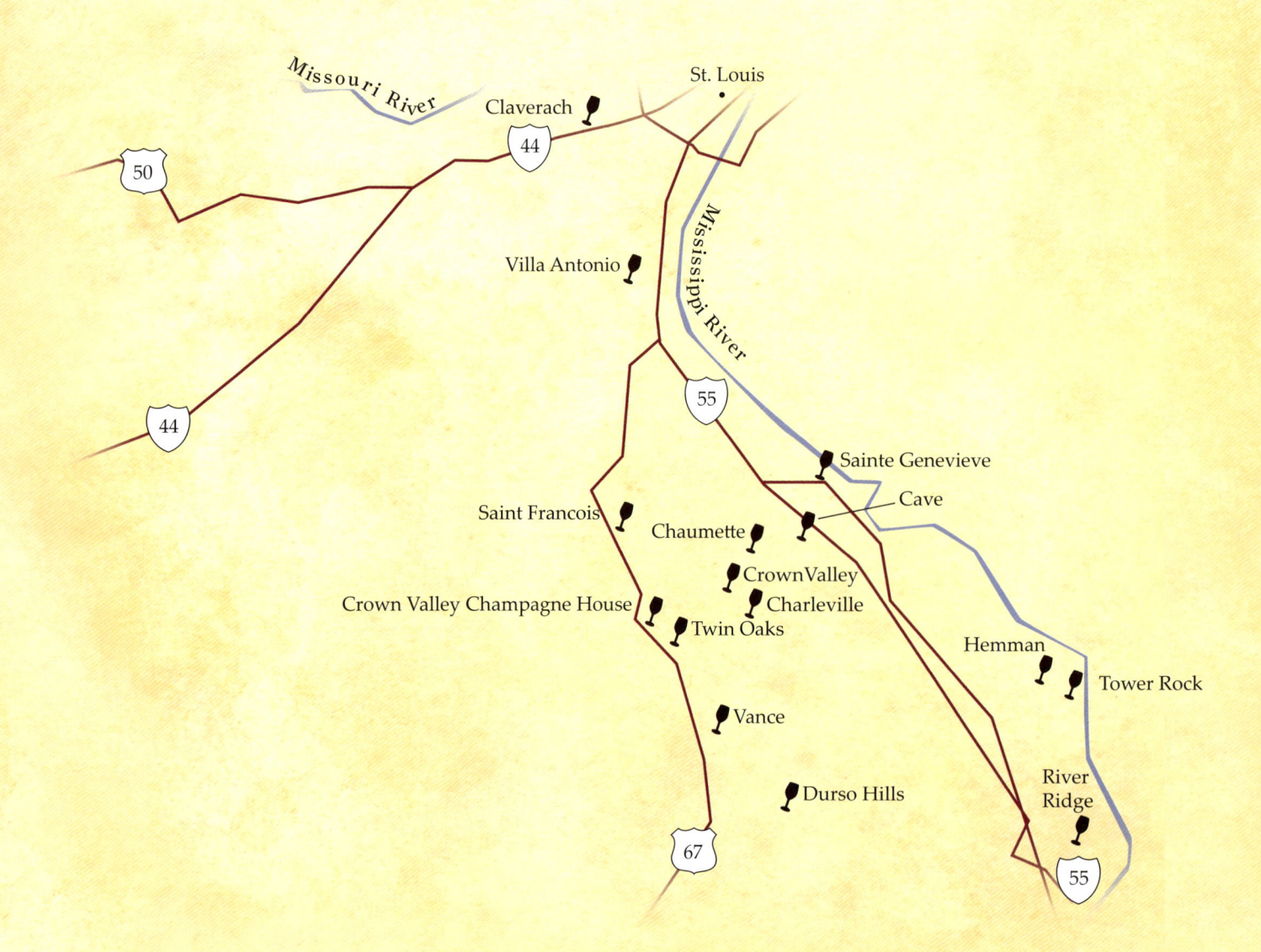

The Southeast region is well known and well loved for its French roots. Originally settled by French immigrants, the region proudly maintains many of its original buildings and French traditions. The most popular towns in the region among wine lovers are Farmington and Sainte Genevieve, with the majority of the region's wineries located in and around Sainte Genevieve.

Located just one hour south of Saint Louis, the town of Sainte Genevieve is the oldest permanent settlement in Missouri and one of the oldest west of the Mississippi River. Its oldest structure, the Bolduc House, was built as a small structure in 1770 at the town's original waterfront location and moved to its present location and expanded in 1785. With its original French-colonial buildings, narrow streets, and enclosed gardens, Sainte Genevieve maintains its original charm and ambiance.

In addition to rich history, Sainte Genevieve offers countless activities for families, friends, and even couples. Visitors are invited to stroll through the town's streets, taking their time to enjoy all the wonder of Sainte Genevieve, stop into each unique specialty shop to browse the fine selection of antiques, crafts, sweets, gifts, and wines, dine in a variety of fine restaurants, and stay overnight in a distinguished bed and breakfast, complete with Old-World charm and the comforts and conveniences of modern living.

Whether for a tour of fine wineries and wine tastings, or a relaxing retreat in the historic charm of Sainte Genevieve, the Southeast region is a great choice for a weekend away from home.

Cave Vineyard

Owners: Marty & Mary Jo Strussion
Winemaker: Marty Strussion
Region: Southeast

Established: 2003
Vineyard Acreage: 14 acres
Annual Production: 1,500 cases

Cave Vineyard

21124 Cave Road
Sainte Genevieve, MO 63670
(573) 543-5284
www.cavevineyard.com

Nestled in the hills of Sainte Genevieve County, Cave Vineyard provides more than just a beautiful view, a delightful atmosphere, and remarkable wines. Cave is the only winery in Missouri offering the unique experience of enjoying award-winning wines inside a natural cave.

Marty and Mary Jo Strussion purchased the property in the late 1990s. Although Marty made wines for personal enjoyment as a young man with his grandfather, he had absolutely no intention of entering the commercial winemaking business when he purchased the land. Instead, the Strussions simply thought that living in the beauty of southeast Missouri would make for a relaxing retirement. When they were presented with the opportunity to purchase their own prime piece of beautiful countryside, they jumped at the chance.

Soon after retiring, the Strussions built a log home on the property and moved into this dream retirement residence. After settling into the home, the Strussions realized that retirement was not for them. Like many other property owners in Sainte Genevieve County, the Strussions quickly discovered that their land was perfect for grape growing.

The Strussions planted their first seven acres of grapevines in 2001 and added seven more acres the following year. After carefully nurturing the vineyard for a couple years, the Strussions harvested their first vintage of grapes in August 2003, which included Chambourcin, Chardonel, Norton, and Traminette varietals.

Using grapes grown in its own vineyard, Cave produces a variety of wines, many of which have received awards for their quality. Visitors can delight in its dry wines, including the Chambourcin, Chardonel Dry, and

Norton; enjoy its off-dry or semi-sweet wines, such as the Blush, Cave Rock Off Dry, and Chardonel Off Dry; or savor its sweet wines of Cave Rock Red, Cave Rock White, Chardonel Late Harvest, and Traminette.

Visitors are always welcome to browse Cave's gift shop or take in the scenic views of the vineyard and rolling hills from the outdoor pavilion. However, a visit to Cave typically starts in its tasting room, which is located over the winery's natural, underground cave wine cellar. After sampling each of Cave's wines and selecting a favorite or two, visitors are invited to take a short walk from the tasting room to Saltpeter Cave for a unique wine tasting experience.

Saltpeter Cave, for which the winery is named, has always been the property's main attraction. The mouth of the cave is an astounding 35 feet in height and 100 feet across, though the ceiling of the cave progressively slopes downward deeper into the cave. It is believed that early French settlers once mined the cave for Saltpeter, which they used to make gunpowder. Today, however, the cave is inhabited primarily by wine enthusiasts seeking a truly unique experience.

ABOVE: Cave carefully hand tends its vineyard to ensure grapes of the highest quality.

ABOVE: Cave's tasting room is located on top of the winery's natural cave wine cellar.

"*Who wouldn't want to own their own cave?!*

— Marty Strussion, Cave Vineyard owner and winemaker, about purchasing the property

Charleville Vineyards

Owners: Jack & Joal Russell
Winemaker: Clyde Gill
Region: Southeast

Established: 2000
Vineyard Acreage: 11 acres
Annual Production: 1,000 cases

In preparation for fulfilling their dream to retire from full-time jobs to grow a few grapes and enjoy life, owners Jack and Joal Russell planted grapevines on their Sainte Genevieve property in 1995. What started as a small retirement project quickly blossomed into a growing business, keeping the Russells much busier than they expected. Although Charleville Vineyards has continued to grow, the Russells have passionately preserved the winery's intimate feel.

In 2003, three years after releasing its first vintage of wines, Charleville opened a small tasting room to allow visitors to enjoy its wines and see where and how they are made. Charleville was a hit with visitors, and additional seating was added to keep up with the winery's popularity. The following year, Charleville expanded by adding a microbrewery, an addition that has proven very successful. In fact, the microbrewery has been so popular that the production of its handcrafted beers has increased every year since 2004.

Using Chardonel, Noiret, and Norton grapes from its vineyard and Chambourcin grapes from a neighboring vineyard, Charleville produces four different Chardonels, a Francois, and a barrel-fermented Norton. For visitors seeking something other than wine, Charleville serves up an assortment of ales, lagers, and seasonal beers from its microbrewery. Even though the microbrewery has only been open for a few short years, some of its offerings have already won critical acclaim.

Still, the Russells knew they could do even more for visitors. In 2005, they renovated a charming log cabin to create a bed and breakfast on the property. In order to preserve the authenticity of the two-bedroom, 1860s cabin while equipping it with today's comfortable amenities, Jack hired and worked with a specialist in log-cabin restorations and furnished the cabin with antiques from the same era. From the cabin, visitors can enjoy a spectacular view of the vineyard and surrounding hillsides.

Charleville, which overlooks the Saline Creek Valley in western Sainte Genevieve County, provides visitors with a rustic and relaxing setting to enjoy great wines. While the tasting room sells sausages and cheeses, customers are always welcome to bring their own snacks from home. Live music throughout the summer only enriches visitors' enjoyment. No matter how large or quickly the winery grows, Charleville will continue to take pride in providing every visitor with the personal attention that the Russells believe makes a true winery experience.

Charleville Vineyards

16937 Boyd Road
Sainte Genevieve, MO 63670
(573) 756-4537
www.charlevillevineyard.com

LEFT: There is no better place to enjoy the beauty of a rainbow than at Charleville.

BELOW: Charleville is well known for its fine handcrafted baskets, as well as its wonderful wines.

BELOW: The winery delights even those visitors far too young to enjoy its fine wines.

" *Penicillin cures, but wine makes people happy.*

— Sir Alexander Fleming, discoverer of penicillin

Chaumette Vineyards & Winery

Owners: Hank & Jackie Johnson
Winemaker: Tony Saballa
Region: Southeast

Established: 2001
Vineyard Acreage: 32 acres
Annual Production: 5,000 cases

Set near the romantic and historic French settlement of Sainte Genevieve is Chaumette Vineyards & Winery, a comprehensive, wine lover's destination, honoring its French predecessors by adopting a 13th-century, French family name. With amenities including a full-service tasting room, a restaurant, fascinating tours, a stylish gift shop, a picturesque chapel, a luxurious spa, and privately-owned villas that can be rented, Chaumette offers a fun yet relaxing atmosphere for all visitors.

Owners Hank and Jackie Johnson purchased the beautiful, 310-acre property in 1990 to serve as a hobby farm after retirement. The beautiful landscape had other plans though. In 1992, the Johnsons planted the property's first grapevines, and their interest in and passion for winemaking naturally evolved. Thanks to the hard work of its skilled winemaker, Tony Saballa, Chaumette produced its inaugural vintage of both Chardonel and Norton wines in 2001, and only two years later, opened its tasting room, delighting visitors with its magnificent wines, elegant yet comfortable setting, and stunning views.

Chaumette is a rarity among new wineries, with so many awards to its name already. The winery offers an amazing selection of whites, from its dry Estate Chardonel to its sweet Late Harvest Chardonel, while still providing such mouthwatering reds as its Assemblage, Bouvet Blend, and Huguenot Red, and a sweet Norton Port. Nevertheless, Chaumette's dry wines are its pride and joy and have really made it one of the state's finest wineries.

Chaumette's French-inspired wines are best enjoyed in its elegantly-decorated tasting room, designed in the style of French-colonial Sainte Genevieve's vertical-log-cabin architecture. The outdoor patio offers breathtaking views of the vineyard and surrounding countryside and often live music. To complement its fine wines, the winery's Grapevine Grill Restaurant delights visitors by serving up a delicious selection of items for lunch and dinner, which include locally-grown produce and locally-raised meats. Additionally, Chaumette hosts weddings and private and corporate events year round, and offers its all-faiths chapel, Saint Vincent's-in-the-Vineyard, for ceremonies.

Chaumette has even more to offer than magnificent wines and fine dining. In 2007, the winery opened Belle Haven Spa, making it the first winery in the Midwest with a full-service resort spa. Belle Haven exclusively uses Caudalíe skincare products, a fine line of all-natural, grape-based products made in the Bordeaux region of France, for the ultimate experience in vinotherapy. Vinotherapy, the latest trend in spa treatment, uses grape and wine mixtures to soothe skin and slow the aging process. The spa also offers therapeutic massages, manicures and pedicures, face and body treatments, a sauna, a hot tub, a heated pool, al fresco poolside dining, private cabanas, and much more.

Also gracing the beautifully-landscaped property is The Villages at Chaumette, a planned development of residential units constructed in the style of the original, 1780s Sainte Genevieve settlement, but with today's most luxurious amenities. While the units are individually privately owned, they are available to rent on a nightly basis. Chaumette is the perfect weekend retreat, whether for a spring bridal party at the spa, a summer wine tasting, a hay ride in the fall, or a romantic winter getaway at The Villages. No matter the season, Chaumette provides visitors an unmatched and unforgettable experience.

Chaumette Vineyards & Winery

24345 State Route WW
Sainte Genevieve, MO 63670
(573) 747-1000
www.chaumette.com

BELOW: Chaumette is the perfect gathering place for friends and family alike.

BELOW: Visitors can enjoy a wonderful view of the vineyard while tasting one of Chaumette's many amazing wines.

A meal without wine is like a day without sunshine.

— Anthelme Brillat-Savarin

Claverach Farm & Vineyards

Claverach Farm & Vineyards

570 South Lewis Road
Eureka, Missouri 63025
(636) 938-4996
www.claverach.com

Owners: Sam & Jean Hilmer, Amanda Hilmer, & Gary Hilmer

Winemaker: Sam Hilmer

Region: Southeast

Established: 2003

Vineyard Acreage: 15 acres

Annual Production: 150 cases

Claverach Farm and Vineyards' owner and winemaker Sam Hilmer believes that the best wines come from the highest-quality raw materials. As a result, he and farm manager Joanna Duley go to great lengths to produce wines at Claverach in a sustainable, environmentally-friendly way. The two take pride in keeping their vineyard and farm in harmony with nature by using natural composts and cover crops to enhance soil vitality and balance. The end result is production of only the most-natural wines, the way wines should be.

Claverach got its start as a small organic farm, growing produce all naturally to sell at local farmers' markets and to restaurants in the Saint Louis area. The first grapevines in its vineyard were planted in 2003 as mere complements to the farming operation, but the quality and popularity of Claverach wines naturally led to an increased emphasis on the vineyard operation. Claverach's organic vineyard is located on the limestone bluffs overlooking its farm in the fertile Meramec River Valley. Using natural techniques, like steeping compost in water and adding this compost tea to the soil, Claverach is able to keep its vineyard healthy and producing the highest-quality grapes possible.

Hilmer's passion for winemaking has deep roots. After completing college, he traveled extensively in Australia, living on organic farms and vineyards. He studied the art of making wine at Louis-Laval Winery in the Hunter Valley and with famed-winemaker Ludwig Mueller at Cassegraine Winery in New South Wales. After returning to the United States, he continued his winemaking studies in the renowned program at the University of California, Davis. For good reason, Hilmer considers himself to be a lifelong student of winemaking.

Claverach, a Welsh term meaning "Clover Fields," takes its name from a 19th-century farm in Clayton owned by the Hilmers' ancestors. Much has remained the same in the 150 years since the first Claverach farm was started. Even the name is still relevant, as clover is used in the vineyard to enhance the fertility of the soil and attract beneficial insects, which help to create distinct, delicious wines.

The grapes at Claverach receive the same care and attention to detail during the winemaking process that they do while still in the vineyard. They are hand harvested only after having reached the perfect point of ripeness, and from these grapes, Claverach then produces small batches of wines, focusing on quality rather than quantity, using small-scale methods, such as basket pressing and gravity racking, and minimal-handling techniques, like sur lie and unfiltered bottling.

The grape varietals grown at Claverach include Cabernet Franc, Cabernet Sauvignon, Chambourcin, Marsanne, Norton, Roussanne, Syrah, and Viognier. Claverach wines are available in stores throughout and around Saint Louis and at the Maplewood Farmers' Market.

With its delightful, all-natural wines, Old-World techniques, and simple approach to growing grapes, Claverach is a wonderful retreat for any wine lover looking to escape the fast pace of life.

ABOVE: Claverach's carefully-tended grapevines provide the foundation for the winery's wonderful wines.

BELOW: Claverach's vineyard is both beautiful and fruitful

Twas Noah who first planted the vine, and mended his morals by drinking its wine.

— Benjamin Franklin

Crown Valley Champagne House

Crown Valley Champagne House
1401 Air Park Drive #4
Farmington, Missouri 63640
(573) 756-7132
www.crownvalleywinery.com

Owner: Joe Scott Senior

Winemaker: Daniel Alcorso

Region: Southeast

Established: 2007

Annual Production: 10,000 cases

Wine lovers are sure to be delighted by Crown Valley Champagne House, the only true champagne house in the Midwest. Owner Joe Scott Senior, who also owns both Crown Valley Winery and Crown Valley Port House, opened the Champagne House in 1997. The winery produces all of Crown Valley's sparkling wines within its state-of-the-art facility, using two different fermentation methods: the traditional Champagne method, or Méthode Champenoise, and the Charmat method, both of which start with the harvest.

The grapes for sparkling wines are picked early in the season, when their sugar content and acidity are low. The low sugar content helps keep the alcohol level low during the initial fermentation process. Later, a second fermentation will boost the alcohol content to its appropriate level. The low acidity helps preserve the wine through the long process of sparkling winemaking. The first fermentation then takes place in the Champagne House's stainless-steel tanks.

After the initial fermentation, the two methods differ. Under the traditional method, the second fermentation takes place in the individual bottles, requires delicate care by a skilled winemaker, and can take up to several years to complete. The Charmat method, on the other hand, is a simpler and faster way to produce large quantities of sparkling wine. Under this method, large batches of wine go through the second fermentation process in huge, glass-lined tanks, and the sparkling wine can be ready to bottle as soon as 90 days after harvest.

The Champagne House gladly offers tours to acquaint its visitors with sparkling winemaking. The 20-minute tour leads visitors first through the fermentation room, where large, stainless-steel tanks hold the young, fermenting wine being produced using the Charmat method and racks support the bottles of fermenting wine being produced using the traditional method. Next, visitors are taken to the bottling room, where impressive automated machinery bottles and puts the finishing touches on each bottle of Crown Valley sparkling wine.

The Champagne House provides guests much more than a lesson in the fine art of producing sparkling wines though. To give visitors only the finest setting for wine tasting, the tasting room highlights rustic Alder cabinetry, stainless-steel countertops, and antique winemaking equipment. The tasting room's design incorporates features of various wineries throughout the world to make for a unique and unforgettable experience.

While in the tasting room, visitors can choose from five different sparkling wines, including Crown Valley's Chardonel Brut, Sparkling Muscato, Sparkling Rosé, Sweet Brachetto, and Traminette Sec, and three different tasting options, ranging from three to ten dollars each. The Champagne House also contains a deli, where visitors can purchase a delightful snack or light meal, and a gift shop that sells almost every Champagne- and wine-related item imaginable, from monogrammed wine glasses to gift baskets.

From its pristine production facility to its charming tasting room, a visit to Crown Valley Champagne House is a one-of-a-kind experience, providing visitors the same high quality that is expected from the Crown Valley name.

ABOVE: Crown Valley wines are a wonderful choice for any occasion.

BELOW: The Sparkling Wine is a refreshing treat for any wine lover.

"
My only regret in life is that I did not drink more Champagne.

— John Maynard Keynes

Crown Valley Winery

Owner: Joe Scott Senior
Winemaker: Daniel Alcorso
Region: Southeast

Established: 1998
Vineyard Acreage: 210
Annual Production: 30,000 cases

Crown Valley Winery
23589 State Route WW
Sainte Genevieve, MO 63670
(866) 207-9463
www.crownvalleywinery.com

In the wine industry, there are certain milestones along the road for every successful winery: the first harvest, the sale of the first bottle of wine, the opening of a tasting room, and the development of a loyal following of wine lovers. Crown Valley Winery owner Joe Scott Senior has managed to do all of these things with such ease and perfection that he has been able to move on to creating other unique milestones, such as the opening of a big cat sanctuary.

Scott built Crown Valley from the ground up. Raised in the town of Coffman, Scott started a ranching operation there in 1984, and in 1998, decided on a whim to plant a small bloc of Chardonel grapevines on the property. Fascinated by the rustic beauty of the vines, he planted even more the following year. As the vines matured and began to produce their first grapes, Scott's thoughts naturally turned to winemaking. In 2000, he and his wife, Loretta Scott, traveled to wineries throughout the world to learn as much as possible about establishing and running a successful winery. The ultimate result was Crown Valley, which has become one of the finest winemaking operations and tourist destinations in Missouri.

Crown Valley serves as the hub of Scott's amazing multipart operation known as "Crown Country." After opening the winery in 2001, Scott also opened both Crown

Valley Port House in Clarksville and Crown Valley Champagne House in Farmington, the latter being the only true champagne house in the Midwest. Those visiting the Port House or the Champagne House can enjoy a tour of the facility, samples of all Crown Valley wines in the tasting room, and a wide selection of wine-related items in the gift shop.

Just as impressive, if not more, is Crown Ridge, a big cat sanctuary in Sainte Genevieve. Opened in 2004, it is now home to five big cats, including a white tiger and a female lion. The mission at Crown Ridge, which also features the elegant Tiger Ridge Restaurant, Tiger Ridge's private banquet facility, and comfortable lodging, is to provide a permanent home and healthy life for exotic cats that have endured abuse or neglect. Visitors to Crown Country can also enjoy a burger and beer while watching a sporting event at Spokes Pub & Grill, or play eighteen holes of golf at Crown Pointe Golf Club, both in Farmington.

ABOVE: Each glass of Crown Valley wine is a finely-crafted masterpiece.

RIGHT: The winery's oak barrels help produce its distinct wines.

Still, Crown Valley itself is nothing short of spectacular. The winery's main building is a beautiful, state-of-the-art structure, featuring such native materials as stone, copper, oak, and reclaimed stained glass. Crown Valley provides tours of its winemaking facility, wine tastings in its tasting room, and cheeses, sausages, and other gourmet snacks to accompany its wines, as well as premium cigars, in its Crown Valley Bistro. There is just as much fun outside at the winery as there is inside. In both the spring and the fall, Crown Valley offers a fun wagon ride throughout the property along special trails, and during the summer, visitors can enjoy live music, barbequed foods, chilled wine, and a dance floor at the winery's Music Pavilion.

In Crown Valley's gift shop, also located in the main building, visitors can find a variety of wine-related gifts and souvenirs, including gift baskets, and an extensive line of specialty food products, including olives, pasta sauces, wine biscuits, flavored coffees, and chocolates. Visitors can also arrange to have a personalized label placed on a bottle of their favorite Crown Valley wine.

Each bottle of Crown Valley wine begins in the vineyard. The winery grows more than a dozen different grape varietals, including Chambourcin, Chardonel, Concord, Frontenac, Mars, Muscat, Norton, Reliance, Rougeon, Shiraz, Traminette, Valvin Muscat, Vignoles, and Viognier. Paying quite a tribute to Missouri's state grape, Crown Valley has become the largest grower of Norton grapes in the entire United States.

Although the winery is less than a decade old, Crown Valley wines are already making a name for themselves by winning medals at wine competitions across the country, and the winery is intent on continuing to spread

BELOW: The beauty of the vineyard and surrounding area delights visitors from near and far.

the Crown Valley name. To promote its best-selling red wine, Sweet Cardinal Red, the winery hosted a tasting at Saint Louis's Busch Stadium during its final year as the home of the Cardinals. Prior to a Cardinals baseball game, fans of at least 21 years of age entering the stadium were provided a free tasting of the delicious wine.

Only an hour from Saint Louis, Crown Valley makes for a wonderful day-long or weekend escape from the city. Adding to its appeal and the variety of entertainment conveniently available to its visitors, Crown Valley offers complimentary shuttle service throughout Crown Country, ensuring that visitors of any age and with any interest have a delightful experience.

ABOVE: A tour of Crown Valley's winemaking facility is both fascinating and fun.

BELOW: With such a wide selection of wines, visitors are sure to find a perfect match for their taste.

Throw away the vintage charts and invest in a corkscrew. The best way to learn about wine is the drinking.

— Alexis Lichine

Durso Hills Vineyard & Winery

Owners: Ron & Kay Durso
Winemaker: Ron Durso
Region: Southeast

Established: 2005
Vineyard Acreage: 2 acres
Annual Production: 400 cases

Durso Hills
Vineyard & Winery

110 North Harding Street
Marquand, Missouri 63655
(573) 783-8324
www.dursohills.com

Durso Hills Vineyard & Winery is a very small, family-owned winery with a big reputation for producing quality wines. Although Durso Hills is located within the town of Marquand, its vineyard sits peacefully among the rural foothills overlooking both the Marquand and Castor Rivers, providing the town a perfect landscape.

Durso Hills' history began in 2000, when owners Ron and Kay Durso planted just over two acres of grapevines. By 2004, the winemaking process was underway, and in October 2005, the winery sold its first bottle of wine. In doing so, Durso Hills became Madison County's first commercial winery.

The wine list at Durso Hills is defined by quality, not quantity. Its 2003 Norton and 2004 Norton each took home a medal at the 2007 Missouri Wine Competition, the 2004 being awarded a gold medal. Durso Hills also produces a sweet red made from Chambourcin grapes and a handful of whites ranging from dry and off-dry to semi-sweet and sweet.

Durso Hills' production facility, tasting room, and gift shop are found in a historic, 100-year-old frame house on a beautiful tree-lined street in the heart of Marquand. In times past, the old building housed the town's local country doctor and his pharmacy, but today it provides a delightful setting for visitors looking to enjoy one of Durso Hills' fine wines and browse its gift shop for memorable gifts and souvenirs. The winery's front porch offers fresh air and a lovely view of the town park.

While Durso Hills provides visitors the same quiet, small-town charm found throughout the rest of Marquand, those looking for excitement can still surely find it during Pioneer Days in late September, when the town celebrates with music, crafts, antiques, food, and wine tasting, and on Harvest Day, when family and friends gather in Durso Hills' vineyard to pick and crush Norton grapes for use in its wines. Whether celebrating with the joyful town of Marquand or enjoying a quiet day of fine wine tasting at the winery, a visit to Durso Hills will surely delight anyone.

ABOVE: Despite the use of modern machinery, fine wines still require a fine winemaker.

ABOVE: North Harding Street is a historic and beautiful location for Durso Hills' tasting room and gift shop.

ABOVE: Durso Hills' vineyard is as beautiful and peaceful as the Castor River and rolling hills that it overlooks.

"*The discovery of a wine is of greater moment than the discovery of a constellation. The universe is too full of stars.*

— Benjamin Franklin

Hemman Winery

Owners: Al & Dorothy Hemman, Doug & Bonnie Hemman, & Corey & Lisa Hemman
Winemakers: Al Hemman, Doug Hemman, & Corey Hemman

Region: Southeast
Established: 2003
Vineyard Acreage: 2 acres
Annual Production: 850 cases

Although young, Hemman Winery has already become a pride and joy of the historic town of Brazeau. Established in 1819, the town still delights visitors who can find many of its original buildings still standing. Bringing together its new tradition of winemaking with the town's historic charm, Hemman is a wonderful destination for any visitor.

The tradition of making delicious, homestyle wines has been passed down through the Hemman family from generation to generation. Al Hemman learned the art of winemaking from his mother, and in order to keep the tradition alive, taught his sons Doug and Corey. Throughout the small town of Brazeau, word of the Hemmans' winemaking abilities spread, and family and friends urged Al to start a winery and share the family's sweet wines with others. After years of indecision, the Hemman family finally decided that the time was right, and they found the perfect site for the winery in a building that once housed a family-owned country store in the mid 1800s. The Hemmans transformed the country store, which had been closed for three decades, into the winery that exists today. Since 2003, the Hemmans have shared with hundreds of visitors each year the same wines that they once produced solely for special family occasions.

Completely family owned and operated, Hemman specializes in handcrafted, sweet and semi-sweet wines. In addition to the winemaking facility, the former country store is also home to the winery's tasting room and gift shop. Having kept much of its original, 19th-century appearance, Hemman allows visitors to travel back in time while tasting its wines. No matter the weather, Hemman's wine garden is a delicious retreat, where visitors, wine glass in hand, can cozy up to the fireplace in cool weather for an intimate conversation or sit back and laugh while enjoying the live music played every second weekend of the month from May though October.

Hemman wines are as unique as the winery's history. In addition to its fantastic grape wines, Hemman produces many unique, sweet and semi-sweet wines from other fruits, such as squash, rhubarb, and pumpkin. The winery is careful not to trade quality for uniqueness though. Several of its wines have been recognized for excellence in several local wine competitions, like its estate-bottled Blackberry, which was awarded a bronze medal at the Missouri Wine Competition.

Hemman invites visitors to spend an entire afternoon, or even just an hour or two, sampling complementary wines in the tasting room, browsing the gift shop, or relaxing on the porch with a bottle of wine and a plate of sausages and cheeses. In the words of the Hemman family, "A day in the country is worth a month in town."

Hemman Winery

13022 Highway C
Brazeau, Missouri 63737
(573) 824-6040
www.hemmanwinery.com

ABOVE: Hemman's fine wines bring visitors nothing but smiles.

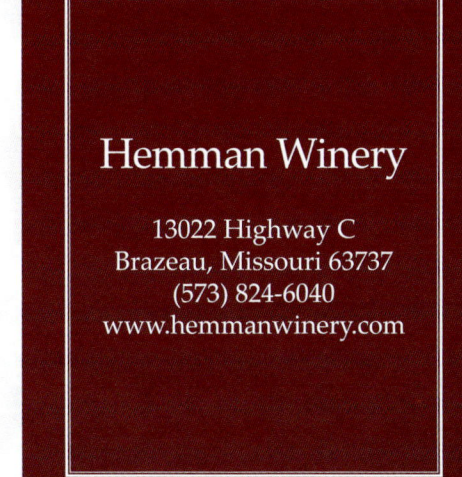

ABOVE: Visitors are always welcome to enjoy the fun and inviting atmosphere at Hemman.

RIGHT: The winery offers live music every second weekend from May through October.

"Wine ... constant proof that God loves us and loves to see us happy.

— Benjamin Franklin

River Ridge Winery

Owners: Jerry & Joannie Smith
Winemaker: Jerry Smith
Region: Southeast

Established: 1994
Vineyard Acreage: 7 acres
Annual Production: 2,700 cases

In the hills overlooking the Mississippi River, visitors can find a century-old farmhouse set in front of a flourishing, well-maintained vineyard. This is River Ridge Winery, where owner and winemaker Jerry Smith has been making fantastic wines since 1994.

In 1980, Jerry purchased an 80-acre farm and began planting grapevines. After meeting and marrying wife and owner Joannie Smith in February 1993, the couple took on the task of refurbishing an old farmhouse on the property into the winery's main building. After a year and a half of hard work, on September 17, 1994, the Smiths opened River Ridge's doors for business.

Since the opening of the winery, the Smiths have continued to work year in and year out adding to the winery's already-impressive offerings. Over the years, River Ridge has seen such improvements as a new production facility; the Fermentation Room Café, where wonderful meals are prepared to order from fresh ingredients; an outdoor pavilion for warm-weather enjoyment; and a two-tiered patio outside the winery, complete with a fire pit. Also, in order to satisfy the great demand by visitors for the opportunity to stay overnight on the beautiful property, a small cabin located on the property was expanded and reopened as Little Log Cabin, River Ridge's own overnight accommodations.

—135—

While the winery's facilities are impressive, its wines are still its pride and joy. Keller Ford, who took the reins as general manager and assistant winemaker in 2003, works with Jerry to lead the River Ridge staff of 15 employees in producing the best wines that its rich Missouri soil can offer. From River Ridge come the very fine wines of Chardonel, Chardonnay, Sauvignon Blanc, Vignoles, and Viognier.

The winery offers visitors the opportunity to taste its wines almost every day of the year. Visitors should plan to spend an afternoon in the beauty of River Ridge, where they can hike a short distance to the vineyard or discover the tranquility of a nearby pond. As the day passes and appetites grow, a relaxing meal can be enjoyed in the winery's dining room, pavilion, or anywhere else on the winery's property, and the River Ridge gift shop features a great selection of fun gifts, wine accessories, and gourmet foods. Additionally, from September through December, visitors can browse the Smiths' Yule Log Cabin Christmas shop just four miles from the winery. As visitors to River Ridge can attest, the Smiths' motto is quite true: "Come as a customer, leave as a friend."

River Ridge Winery

850 County Road 321
Commerce, Missouri 63742
(573) 264-3712
www.riverridgewinery.com

LEFT: River Ridge's tasting room maintains the winery's beautiful, country feel.

BELOW: The vineyard is carefully maintained to ensure high-quality River Ridge wines.

A man should not refuse a little wine when it is pressed upon him.

— Yoshida Kenko

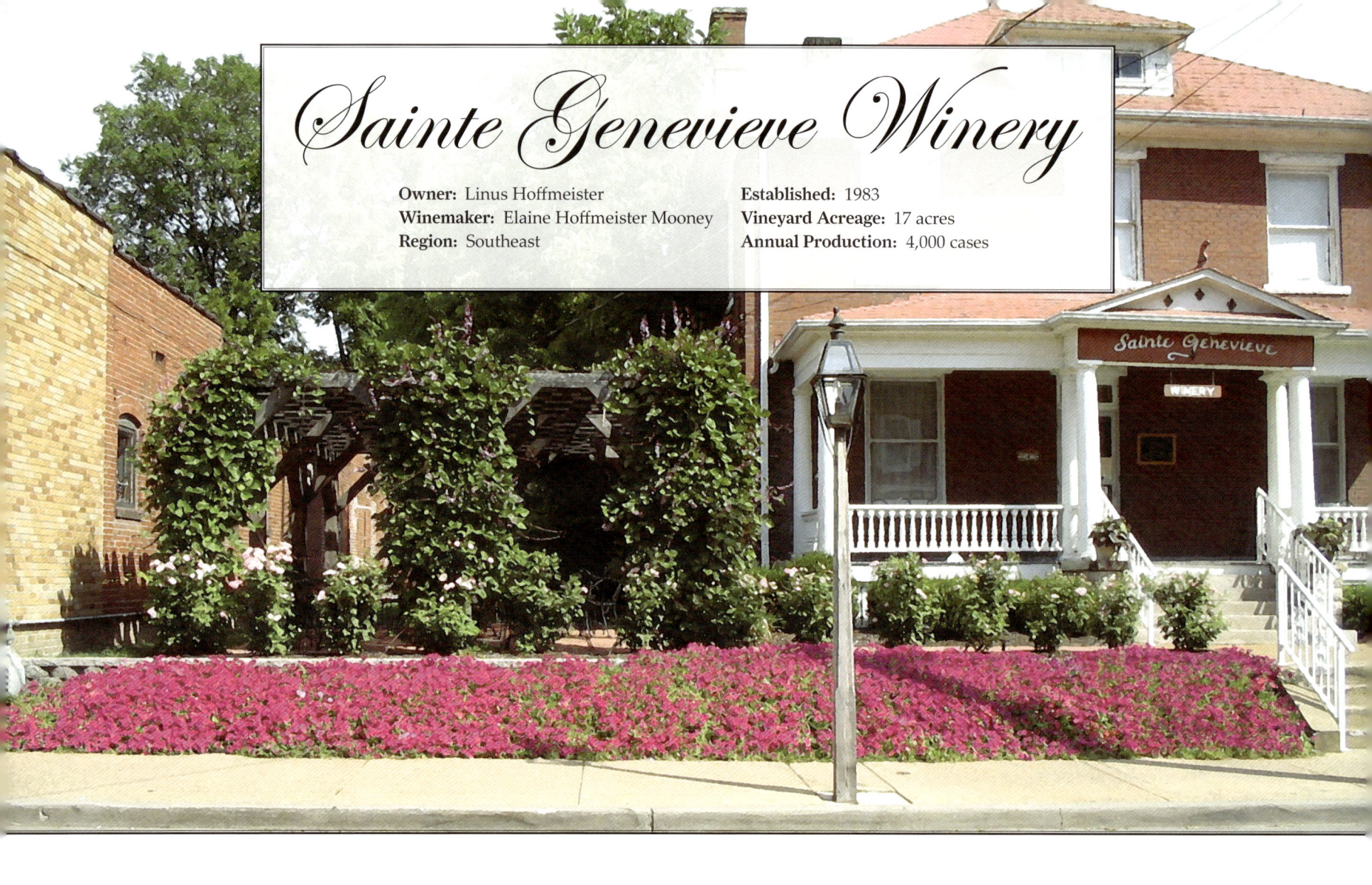

Sainte Genevieve Winery

Owner: Linus Hoffmeister
Winemaker: Elaine Hoffmeister Mooney
Region: Southeast

Established: 1983
Vineyard Acreage: 17 acres
Annual Production: 4,000 cases

Sainte Genevieve Winery's rich history and amazing wines provide visitors the feeling of a special connection with traditional French culture. The winery is located amid the restaurants, bed and breakfasts, and antique shops of historic downtown Sainte Genevieve, which is the oldest French settlement west of the Mississippi River.

The roots of the winery were planted in 1983, when owner Linus Hoffmeister, together with his wife Mary Hoffmeister, began producing wine on their family farm. Within only two years, the Hoffmeisters purchased and renovated a beautiful, turn-of-the-century home to accommodate the winery's growth. The 5,000-square-foot structure is now home to Sainte Genevieve Winery's tasting room, gift shop, and lovely bed and breakfast. The winery is quite a family affair, with the Hoffmeisters' daughter, Elaine Hoffmeister Mooney, having taken over as winemaker. Elaine received a degree in enology from California State University-Fresno in 1999, and is now doing her part to help the winery continue its tradition of producing award-winning wines.

Sainte Genevieve Winery is committed to quality rather than quantity, producing award-winning, handcrafted wines in small lots to suit every visitor's palate and pocketbook. The winery's Blackberry wine, for example, definitely fits the bill, winning numerous awards year after year, including a silver medal at the 2004 New World International Wine Competition, a silver medal at the 2004 Missouri Wine Competition, a bronze medal at the 2004 Indy International Wine Competition, and a gold medal at the 2004 Tasters Guild Wine Competition. Sainte Genevieve Winery's wine list is as expansive as it is exquisite, offering a wide variety of both grape wines, including its Amoureaux, Beauvais, Bolduc, Concord, Estate Vignoles, Lady Genevieve, LaRose Rosé, Sainte Gemme, Seyval Blanc, Traminette,

Valle Rhine, and Vidal Blanc, and its other fruit wines of Apple, Apricot, Blackberry, Blueberry, Cherry, Christmas Plum, Cranberry, Elderberry, Pear, Red Currant, Red Raspberry, and Strawberry.

On a peaceful summer afternoon, visitors can take in the beauty of Sainte Genevieve Winery's vineyard from its outdoor seating area under the grape arbor. The arbor was handbuilt by Linus from lumber collected in the forest on the property. The live entertainment every Saturday in May, June, September, and October makes for an enjoyable afternoon, and a plate of local sausages and cheeses is an excellent complement to a Sainte Genevieve Winery wine.

For a great weekend getaway, visitors can enjoy a night's stay at the lovely Chateau Sainte Genevieve, located on the second floor of the winery's main building. The Chateau has been completely renovated in a luxurious, Queen-Anne décor and provides home-away-from-home charm and elegance. In addition to a full breakfast each morning, visitors receive a special private wine tasting and a bottle of Sainte Genevieve Winery's own wine. Life does not get much better than at Sainte Genevieve Winery.

Sainte Genevieve Winery

245 Merchant Street
Sainte Genevieve, MO 63670
(800) 398-1298
www.saintegenevievewinery.com

ABOVE: Sainte Genevieve is the perfect setting for enjoying great wines with family and friends.

RIGHT: The winery's luscious beauty keeps visitors coming back time and time again.

"*Wine, one sip of this will bathe the drooping spirits in delight beyond the bliss of dreams. Be wise and taste.*

— *John Milton*

Saint Francois Vineyard & Winery

Saint Francois Vineyard & Winery

1669 Pine Ridge Trail
Park Hills, Missouri 63601
(573) 431-4294
www.stfrancoiswinery.com

Owner: Ed Daugherty
Winemaker: Ed Daugherty
Region: Southeast
Established: 1997
Vineyard Acreage: 9 acres
Annual Production: 1,000 cases

Situated in the beautiful Saint Francois Range, Saint Francois Vineyard & Winery provides a great setting for a relaxing yet joyful day filled with fun, friends, and of course, wines. The winery's exquisite wines and pleasant atmosphere make any visit an unforgettable experience.

Saint Francois has been both growing grapes and raising nursery grapevines for nearly two decades, but the same passion for grapevines and wines that existed when the winery was established is still present today. The winery evolved from Saint Francois's original grapevine nursery business, which began on a commercial level in 1992. As the main vines continued to grow to supply cuttings for propagation, the number of grapes produced by the vines also increased. Initially, the grapes were harvested and sold to other Missouri wineries. In 2005 though, after eight years of careful planning and construction, Saint Francois's winery was finally complete and ready to make wines from its grapes. Today, visitors enjoy the fine wines produced from the grapes harvested in the winery's vineyard and processed in its winemaking facility.

From its Pine Ridge Red, a delicious addition to any Sangria or party punch, to its Tickle Me Pink, which pairs well with cheeses, sausages, and other finger foods, Saint Francois produces a wide array of dry, semi-dry, and sweet wines to please any palate. The winery uses Chambourcin, Chardonel, Cynthiana, and Traminette grapes to produce its fun and fruity wines.

Saint Francois provides complimentary wine tastings in a relaxed, country setting. Following a tasting, visitors often enjoy browsing the winery's gift shop or simply sitting back to enjoy their favorite wines and snacks while admiring the views from the peaceful outdoor patio. To accommodate those unable to leave their work at the office, Saint Francois even provides free wireless internet service.

Saint Francois is unique in its production of wines "from stem to stemware." It nurtures and raises nursery grapevines, grows grapes on the vines, processes the grapes into wines, bottles the wines in its bottling facility, and finally, pours its visitors their own glass of Saint Francois wine, all on the same beautiful location. Because of this rarity in the wine industry, Saint Francois has to help others by growing grapevine-planting stock for vineyards across the United States, shipping tens of thousands of starter vines each year. For a behind-the-scenes look at the winery's full operations, visitors are welcome to take a special tour of the nursery, vineyard, and winery.

After an afternoon of tasting and touring at Saint Francois, visitors always leave with a big smile and an even bigger desire to return soon.

LEFT: Saint Francois's remarkable wines all start in its vineyard.

LEFT: Visitors enjoy the relaxing scenery at the winery.

Wine is bottled poetry.
— Robert Louis Stevenson

—140—

Tower Rock Winery

Owners: Bob & Cheryl Breuer
Winemaker: Bob Breuer
Region: Southeast
Established: 2001
Vineyard Acreage: 3 acres
Annual Production: 1,000 cases

Sitting between the Mississippi River and the Ozark Mountains in southern Perry County is Tower Rock Winery, a small, delightful winery serving up great wines and great times. Visitors can enjoy free wine samples in the winery's tasting room and a selection of unique, wine-related items in its gift shop. Just outside the main building are a peaceful garden, a serene lake, and Tower Rock's three-acre vineyard. Whether enjoying the picturesque scenery, relaxing atmosphere, or wonderful wines with family or friends, it does not get any better than at Tower Rock.

Owners Bob and Cheryl Breuer planted the winery's first grapevines in 1997, and Tower Rock began producing high-quality wines as soon as the grapes were harvestable. Less than 10 years after the vines went into the ground, Tower Rock wines were already winning awards. In 2006, the winery entered its wines for the first time in the Missouri Wine Competition and won a medal in each category entered. Even more impressively, its delicious Estate Cynthiana Reserve was awarded "Best of Class" in the reds category and was a finalist for the Governor's Cup, which is awarded to the single best overall wine in Missouri each year. The following year, Tower Rock's Chambourcin won seven medals, including a double gold at the Eastern International Wine Competition and a gold at the American Wine Society Competition. Tower Rock is especially proud of its dry reds, but it also produces a variety of wonderful dry whites and semi-sweet wines.

Tower Rock provides much more than just a great selection of wines. Visitors can also enjoy the atmosphere of the winery's screened porch and the comfortable indoor seating area, where light snacks are served to complement the wines, including locally-made sausages and cheeses. While sipping a glass of their favorite Tower Rock wine, visitors are also always welcome to tour the winery's winemaking facility and see where its next award-winning wines are being fermented and aged.

The beautiful scenery at Tower Rock is a large part of its attraction as well. Aside from the vineyard and surrounding countryside, the winery is only three miles from the majestic Tower Rock. The historic limestone outcropping is slightly less than an acre in size, but towers more than 90 feet above the Mississippi River bed. The winery is also less than three miles from the original Mississippi River Trail, which stretches the length of the river. The Trail is popular among bicyclists, and so is the winery, which welcomes them into its vineyard for a rest during a long day of cycling. Tower Rock clearly has a little something for everyone.

Tower Rock Winery

10769 Highway A
Altenburg, Missouri 63732
(573) 824-5479
www.tower-rock-winery.com

ABOVE: The winery's patio overlooks a beautiful, tranquil lake.

RIGHT: Regardless of where visitors choose to sit, Tower Rock provides fun for all.

"*Beer is made by men, wine by God.*

— Martin Luther

Twin Oaks Vineyard & Winery

Owners: Keith & Karen Hutson
Winemakers: Brian Hutson & Andy Hutson
Region: Southeast

Established: 2007
Vineyard Acreage: 25 acres
Annual Production: 1,300 cases

Twin Oaks
Vineyard & Winery

6470 Highway F
Farmington, Missouri 63640
(573) 756-6500
www.twinoaksvineyard.com

Until spring 2000, Twin Oaks Vineyard & Winery was merely the Hutson family farm. Prior to planting their first grapevines on the property, Keith and Karen Hutson spent years cultivating and nurturing the nutrient-rich soil on their 180-acre farm. In April 2000, the couple made a big change and converted 25 acres of the farm into a vineyard, and Twin Oaks was born.

After six years of the Hutsons carefully tending the grapevines, brothers Andrew Hutson and Brian Hutson made the Hutson family's dream a reality by producing Twin Oaks' first wines, and in May 2007, Twin Oaks opened its tasting room and sold its first bottle of wine. Although Twin Oaks' wine production has quickly grown since that time to more than 1,300 cases annually, special care has been taken to ensure that the quality of its grapes and wines have not suffered. The Hutson family still manages almost every aspect of the vineyard's care, and at harvest time, it is not uncommon to find four generations of Hutsons handpicking grapes for wine production.

Appreciating Twin Oaks' exquisite vineyard is easy for visitors, because the tasting room sits in the middle of the property surrounded by grapevines. The tasting room is quite inviting and features large-screen televisions, beautiful antiques, and a cozy fireplace. Not only may guests indulge in Twin Oaks' wonderful wines, but also in fresh meats, cheeses, crackers, fruits, chocolates, and premium beers.

Twin Oaks' beauty extends outside of its tasting room though. Visitors can enjoy a glass of Twin Oaks wine on the charming porch overlooking the vineyard and tranquil lake or under the winery's nearly-400-year-old oak trees, for which the winery was named. Twin Oaks also features live entertainment on weekends, making it an excellent combination of relaxation and fun. Located only 60 miles from Saint Louis, Twin Oaks makes for a fantastic day or weekend getaway.

ABOVE: The eloquent and inviting tasting room is the perfect place to sip a magnificent glass of Twin Oaks wine while cooling off on a hot summer day.

RIGHT: The winery's outdoor patio is surrounded by well-manicured foliage and overlooks both the vineyard and the lake.

BELOW: Twin Oaks' tasting room and gift shop sit in the middle of the beautiful vineyard.

Wine ... offers a greater range for enjoyment and appreciation than possibly any other purely sensory thing which may be purchased.
— Ernest Hemingway

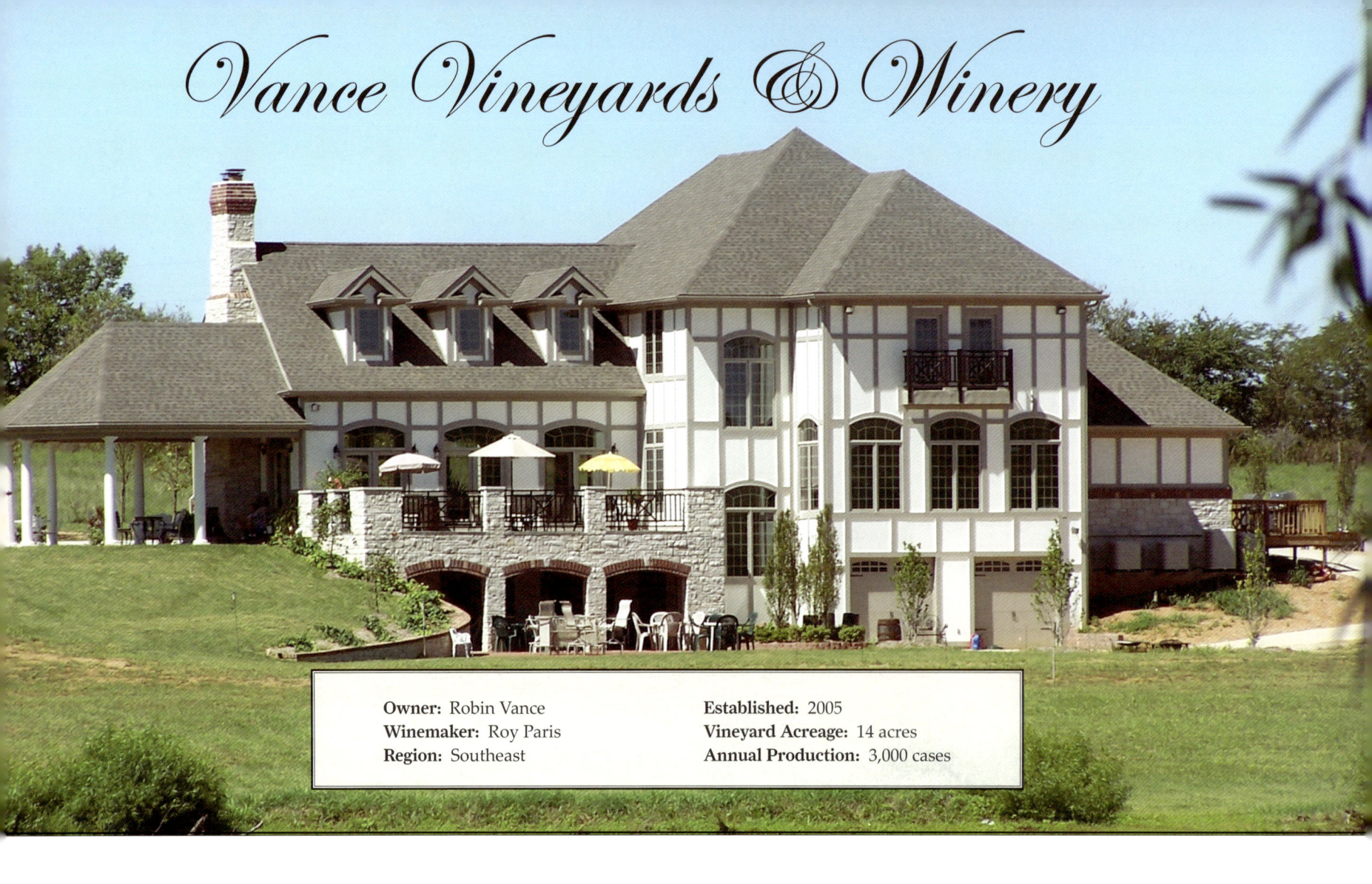

Vance Vineyards & Winery

Owner: Robin Vance
Winemaker: Roy Paris
Region: Southeast

Established: 2005
Vineyard Acreage: 14 acres
Annual Production: 3,000 cases

In the early 1800s, a flood of German immigrants moved westward across the United States in search of a new homeland that would remind them of their beloved "Old Country." Upon seeing the vast, rolling hills and pristine waterways of Madison County in southeast Missouri, they knew they had found it. The immigrants cleared the land, planted crops, and built traditional, German-style homes and outbuildings. One of these immigrants, Frederick Schulte, came to Madison County from Germany at the age of six with his widowed mother. When Schulte grew up, he farmed the land, raised a family on it, and came to be a prominent entrepreneur and citizen in the community.

Today, Schulte is gone, but his legacy is far from forgotten. The "Old Schulte Farm," on what is locally still called "Schulte Lane," though officially named County Road 212, is now home to Vance Vineyards & Winery. The three-story concrete silo that Schulte constructed in the 1800s still stands today. It will soon be converted into a clock tower and serve as the centerpiece of the magnificent landscape surrounding the winery.

Aside from converting Schulte's silo into a clock tower, owner Robin Vance has taken additional steps to maintain Schulte's German heritage on the property. Most significantly, Robin had the winery built in a style of traditional-German architecture. Much more than a tasting room, the main building also houses a banquet and meeting room, a hearth room and piano bar, a gift shop, and numerous balconies and patios from which to enjoy the view. One of Vance's outdoor patios even has a stone fireplace to provide a welcoming and comfortable atmosphere for visitors to enjoy a bottle of Vance wine while gazing over the winery's tranquil lake.

As if Vance's beautiful setting and great wines were not enough, the winery also boasts the first-rate yet affordable

Twisting V Grille. The restaurant serves up a wide range of foods from meats, such as seafood and lamb, to salads, desserts, and soups. Vance's expansive facility allows those staying for dinner the choice of dining in the hearthroom, on the terrace, or on the upper balcony. Almost any wine could be enjoyed in such beautiful settings, but Vance produces only wines of remarkable quality made from the Catawba, Chambourcin, Chardonel, Chardonnay, Marquis, Norton, Riesling, Traminette, Vanessa, Venus, and Vignoles grapes grown in its vineyard.

Although construction of a state-of-the-art production facility and testing laboratory was recently completed, Vance wines do not owe their quality to technology, but rather to winemaker Roy Paris. With more than 30 years of experience producing wines, his skill assures that every bottle is worthy of the winery's label. With everything from dry to sweet and red to white, visitors are sure to find a Vance wine to suit their taste.

LEFT: Vance's well-kept vineyard is a tribute to the winemaking philosophy that fine wines start with fine vines.

BELOW: The view from Vance's tasting room is breathtaking and provides visitors with feelings of peace and tranquility.

Vance Vineyards & Winery

1522 Madison 212
Fredericktown, Missouri 63645
(573) 783-8800
www.vancevineyards.com

" *A bottle of good wine, like a good act, shines ever in the retrospect.*

— Robert Louis Stevenson

Villa Antonio Winery

Owners: Antonio & Fernanda Polesel

Winemaker: Antonio Polesel

Region: Southeast

Established: 2001

Vineyard Acreage: 10 acres

Villa Antonio Winery

3662 Linhorst Road
Hillsboro, Missouri 63050
(636) 475-5008
www.villaantoniowinery.com

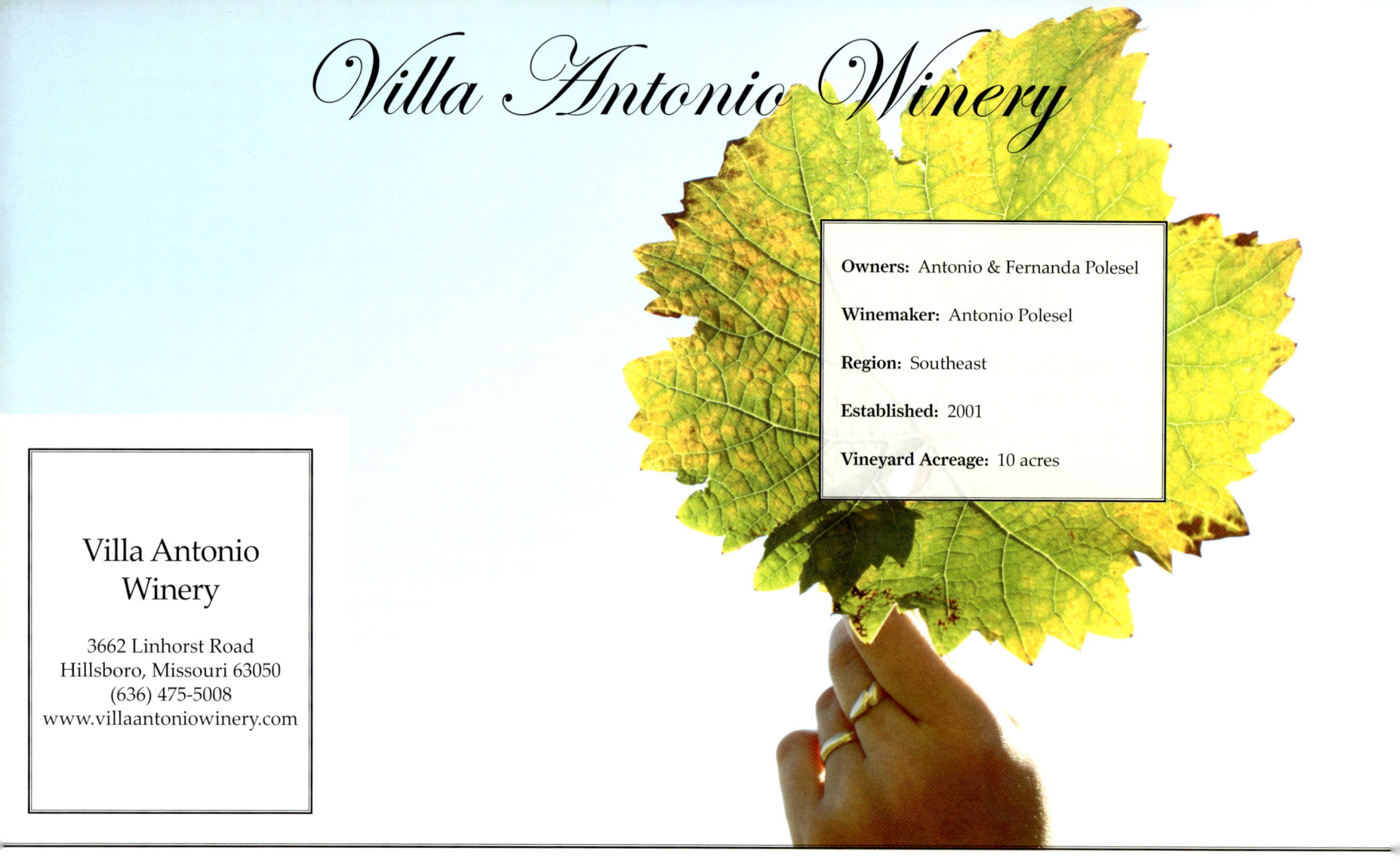

Romantic lakeside and vineyard views set the stage for a delightful experience at Villa Antonio Winery. Found in the small town of Hillsboro, the winery offers a picturesque retreat where visitors can relax in the private serenity of its beautiful vineyard and historic cabin, all while enjoying some great wines and foods.

Villa Antonio is a family-owned winery located close enough to Saint Louis to make for a wonderful day trip. The winery is housed in a 19th-century log cabin, which offers visitors a comfortable and elegant tasting room in which to try its wines. Outside the cabin, Villa Antonio provides a wonderfully-landscaped selection of seating areas, including a large deck, grape arbor, four-seasons pavilion, and beautiful patio. Visitors to the winery on weekends and most holidays from April through October happily find the air filled with live music and laughter, and picnic baskets are always welcome, as Villa Antonio wines are well complemented by a variety of snacks.

The Italian heritage of owners Antonio and Fernanda Polesel is reflected in the winery's foods, wines, and warm hospitality. Antonio, who is also Villa Antonio's skilled winemaker, learned the art of winemaking from his father while growing up in the Veneto region of northeastern Italy. Since that time, he has continued to refine his skills in producing fine Italian-style wines from the native-American and European-American hybrid grape varietals that flourish in Missouri. From the hands of its skilled winemaker come Villa Antonio's fine wines of Chambourcin, Chardonel, Norton, and Seyval Blanc, to name a few.

While Antonio handles the winemaking, Fernanda is in charge of the winery's food preparation. Using only the freshest produce and meats available, she lovingly prepares wonderful Italian dishes. Villa Antonio's light lunch menu includes antipasto, cheeses, fruits, toasted ravioli, desserts, and pastries, each of which is delicious with its wines. For those with a bigger appetite, the winery offers a wonderful seven-course dinner of authentic Italian cuisine in a semiformal setting, where visitors all begin dining at the same time to enjoy the experience together. Each dinner is finished off with a specially-prepared selection of pastries and other desserts.

Italy is famous for its fine foods and world-class wines. Keeping true to its owners' heritage, Villa Antonio brings a little piece of Italy right here to Missouri. Wine lovers searching for a unique Italian experience will find it in Hillsboro at Villa Antonio.

ABOVE: Fine grapes go into each of the winery's Italian-style wines.

BELOW: Each Villa Antonio wine is aged for just the right amount of time for highest quality.

"*I have lived temperately....I double the doctor's recommendation of a glass and a half of wine each day and even treble it with a friend.*

— *Thomas Jefferson*

West Region

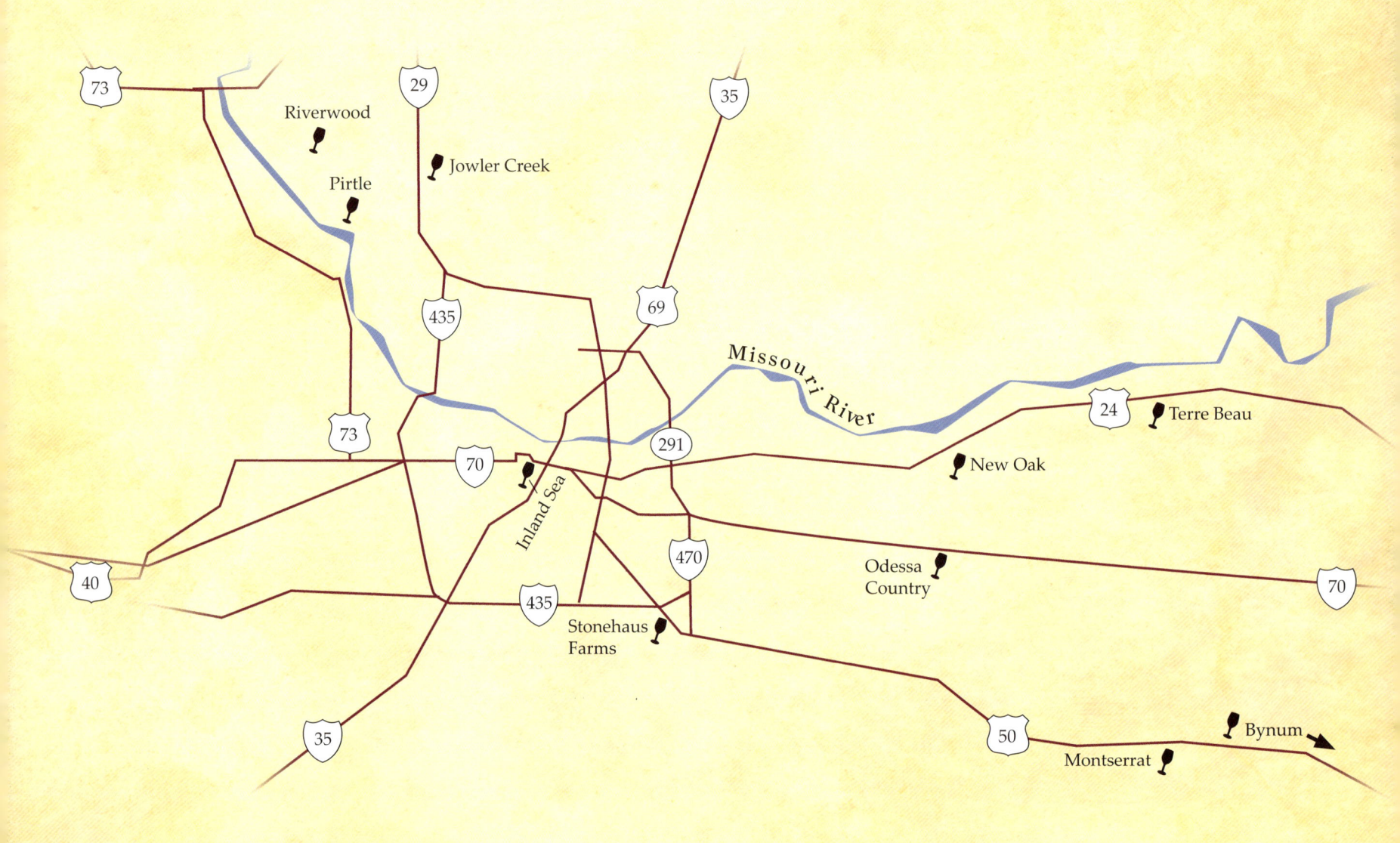

The West region encompasses the Kansas City area east to U.S. Highway 65. In addition to the wonderful wines produced by the region's wineries, visitors to the region can enjoy great entertainment and culture in Kansas City, as well as the beauty of numerous surrounding lakes and parks.

Kansas City has almost everything imaginable to delight any visitor. The Kansas City Chiefs football team, Kansas City Royals baseball team, and Kansas City Wizards soccer team provide entertainment year round for sports lovers. For a full day of family fun, the Kansas City Zoo features nearly 1,000 animals, and the Worlds of Fun and Oceans of Fun theme parks offer a combined 235 acres of enjoyment. Visitors who enjoy history can certainly find it at Union Station Kansas City. The city also offers plenty of attractions centered around the arts, such as The Nelson-Atkins Museum of Art, dining and shopping opportunities, especially at the Country Club Plaza, and nightlife.

The region also offers outdoor enthusiasts a refuge from the busy city life. With at least seven large parks, some as large as 1,000 acres, visitors can enjoy all kinds of recreational activities, including hiking, bird watching, horseback riding, or just relaxing on a picnic with loved ones.

Still, the region's wineries are not to be forgotten. From Inland Sea Wines, set in a historic downtown district of Kansas City, to New Oak Vineyards, offering beautiful countryside relaxation, the West region really does have something for everyone.

Bynum Winery

Owners: Floyd & Maxine Bynum
Winemaker: Floyd Bynum
Region: West

Established: 1989
Vineyard Acreage: 6 acres
Annual Production: 500 cases

As visitors travel through the countryside of western Missouri, they may stumble upon the red barn and quaint vineyard of Bynum Winery, just east of Kansas City, near the town of Lone Jack. The Bynum family has a long and rich history in the Lone Jack area, and the winery is a reflection of the family's heritage. The Bynums were among the earliest settlers of the area that would later become Lone Jack, arriving in 1836. Owner and winemaker Floyd Bynum's great-grandmother was an Osage Indian who married a Bynum in the 1800s, and before Prohibition, Floyd's great-great-uncle, George Shawhan, was the maker of Lone Jack's famous Shawhan Whiskey.

Floyd kept George's tradition of bringing great joy through great drinks alive by opening Bynum Winery in 1989. Winemaking was a natural fit for Floyd, who was educated and has a professional background in agriculture, chemistry, and administration and supervision. Prior to establishing Bynum, Floyd worked in food chemistry and education administration, and also managed Midi Vineyard from 1982 to 1988, where he acquired much of his knowledge of the winemaking process and wine industry as a whole. Floyd calls on all of this education and experience in operating both Bynum and the family farm on a daily basis.

Bynum's vineyard spans six acres, with plans to add 30 more acres of grapevines over time. Additionally, the family farm has an orchard of apples, cherries, peaches, pears, and a variety of berries. The wide array of fruits grown allows Bynum to create some very enjoyable and unique wines, such as its Concord, Foxy Red, Miss Meadow, Vidal Blanc, and White Dove.

The philosophy at Bynum is that wine should be savored and enjoyed at meal time, and the relaxed atmosphere at the winery is perfect for savoring and enjoying all that life has to offer. Visitors are welcome to sample each of Bynum's wines in the tasting room or lounge in the small picnic area outside to enjoy a bottle of wine, a snack, and the beautiful scenery. Visitors are encouraged to tour the winery and to pick up a special souvenir in Bynum's gift shop. During the growing season, Bynum also sells fresh vegetables grown by Floyd on the family farm, allowing visitors to purchase almost everything necessary for that down-home, Missouri meal, complete with fresh vegetables and delicious wines. Bynum is the ideal choice for any visitor looking for great wines in a beautiful and laidback atmosphere.

Bynum Winery

13520 South Sam Moore Road
Lone Jack, Missouri 64070
(816) 566-2240

ABOVE: Bynum carefully tends its vineyard from the planting of the vines to the picking of the grapes.

BELOW: Bynum's Vignoles grapes are the product of a well-maintained vineyard.

" *Wine … is the only beverage that feeds the body, soul, and spirit of man and at the same time stimulates the mind.*

— Robert Mondavi

Inland Sea Wines

Owners: Kerry Amigoni & John Poston
Winemakers: Michael Amigoni & John Poston
Region: West

Established: 2006
Vineyard Acreage: 4 acres
Annual Production: 600 cases

Inland Sea Wines

1600 Genessee, Suite 160
Kansas City, Missouri 64102
(888) 984-9463
www.inlandseawines.com

Inland Sea Wines takes its name from a number of different geographically-historic references. In the Cretaceous Period, spanning from approximately 145 million to 65 million years ago, shallow seas covered the entire area, forming the limestone parent material for its vineyard. Much more recently, Native-American inhabitants referred to the rolling prairies as a vast "sea of grass." Today, Inland Sea sits at the meeting point of the Kansas and Missouri Rivers in a historic district of Kansas City. While its name comes from references to the area's geographical history, its reputation comes from its delicious wines, urban setting, and fun atmosphere.

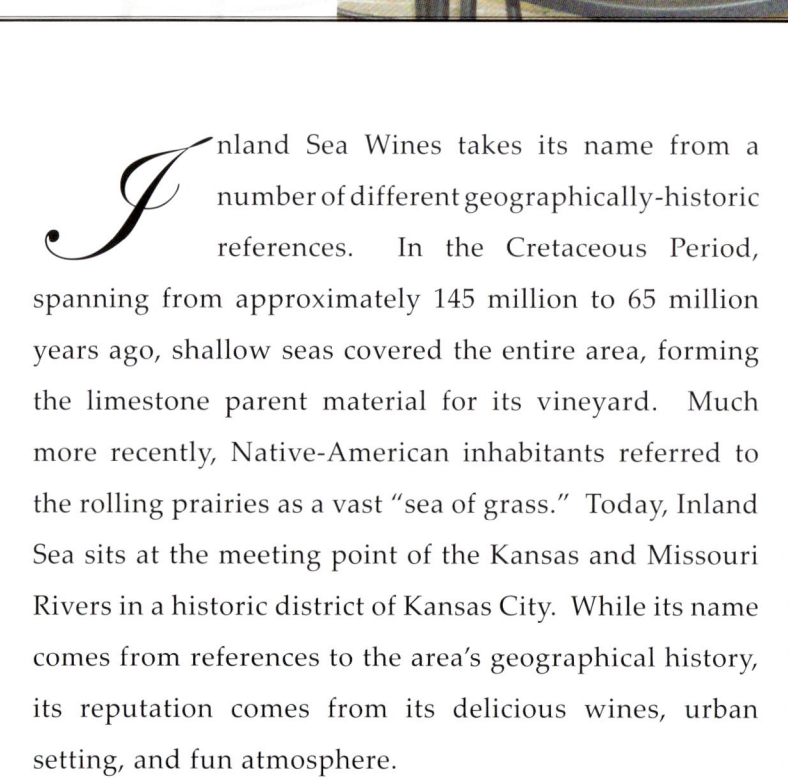

Inland Sea produces its wines from grapes grown at Amigoni Family Vineyards, which is located in Centerview, 30 miles east of Kansas City. Previously a grazing space for cattle, the land is now the site of three flourishing vineyard blocs and is characterized by a silty, sandy loam with black limestone about six feet below the surface, created by the shallow seas covering the land many millions of years ago.

In 2006, winery owners Kerry Amigoni and Michael Poston established Inland Sea and began looking in the West Bottoms of Kansas City for the perfect urban location for the winery. The West Bottoms served as an important industrial center in the 20th century and is now one of the oldest parts of the city. When the owners found the historic Livestock Exchange Building on Genessee Street, they knew that their search was over. Revered as the largest livestock-exchange building in the world at the time of its completion in 1911, the building was renovated into commercial properties in 1991 and is now the home of Inland Sea.

Inland Sea produces four varietals of wine under its

Inland Sea and Sea Turtle labels, including Cabernet Franc, Chardonnay, Malbec, and Viognier. Inland Sea's inaugural red, the 2006 Inland Sea Cabernet Franc, has been described as harmonious, pure, and velvety and has quickly become a house favorite. Visitors also enjoy the Viognier, a barrel-fermented white with a sweet fragrance reminiscent of apricot and tropical fruits.

Just as impressive as its fine, handcrafted wines is Inland Sea's dedication to giving back to its community. The winery donates a portion of every sale to a pair of charitable organizations that go a long way in making the world a better place: the Nature Conservancy and the Batten Disease Support and Research Association. The first of these organizations helps preserve millions of acres of natural habitat around the world, including some of the prairies near the winery, while the second provides support for research of this degenerative neurological disorder and for the families of children and young adults with the disorder. In so many ways, Inland Sea strives to bring satisfaction to the lives of all whom it touches.

ABOVE: Like grapes straight from the vine, Inland Sea is a fresh, new winery for visitors to enjoy.

BELOW: The winery is located in an urban setting, giving visitors a unique experience.

ABOVE: Inland Sea wines are made from only the finest grapes.

" *Wine ... the intellectual part of the meal.*

— Alexandre Dumas

Jowler Creek Winery

Owners: Jason & Colleen Gerke
Winemakers: Jason & Colleen Gerke
Region: West

Established: 2006
Vineyard Acreage: 6 acres
Annual Production: 550 cases

Jowler Creek Winery
16905 Jowler Creek Road
Platte City, Missouri 64079
(816) 935-9471
www.jowlercreek.com

Like love, wine is definitely something to be shared. Jason and Colleen Gerke, owners of Jowler Creek Winery, could not agree more.

The Gerkes first started making wine together as a hobby in their Kansas City basement. Before long, their love of winemaking blossomed into something more. In 2003, the couple decided to put their skills to the test. They moved to a scenic, 15-acre property along historic Jowler Creek in Platte County and began planning their very own boutique winery. The following spring, the Gerkes put their plans into motion, planting 250 Norton grapevines. Soon, they expanded the small vineyard to include three more varietals: Cabernet Franc, Traminette, and Vignoles. By 2006, the grapes were ready for pressing, and Jowler Creek's first vintage of wines hit the shelves in 2007. The Gerkes' dream had become a reality.

From the start, the Gerkes had but one goal in mind: to make wines that are fun to drink and easy to pair with the cuisine served in their hometown of Kansas City. This goal is reflected in everything from Jowler Creek's rustic raccoon logo to its unique and flavorful wines, including the aptly-named Critter Cuvée. Jowler Creek produces

ABOVE: Each member of Jowler Creek's Grand Cru club gets to "adopt a vine."

two dry wines (Cabernet Franc and Norton), three semi-sweet wines (Critter Cuvée, Traminette, and Vignoles), and two dessert wines (Nort and Premium Sweet Vignoles). Although Jowler Creek is a young winery, with only one vintage under its belt, the character and high quality of its wines indicate a bright future ahead.

Jowler Creek wines can be found in fine restaurants and wine shops across the greater-Kansas City area, and wine lovers will soon be able to enjoy its wines onsite in its new tasting room. Jowler Creek also offers two wine club memberships: the Creek Club and the Grand Cru. Both allow members to have its newest wines delivered straight to their door every three months, before the wines even hit store shelves. Additionally, Grand Cru members receive other benefits, such as having their very own "adopted vine" in the vineyard, admission to special winery events, and more.

Although Jowler Creek is still young, its casual, country atmosphere and fun and tasty wines will surely be enjoyed for many years to come.

ABOVE: Jowler Creek wines owe much of their quality to the grapes that go into them.

BELOW: The winery's vineyard brings a smile to any face.

> *Wine had such ill effects on Noah's health that it was all he could do to live 950 years.*
>
> — Will Rogers

Montserrat Vineyards

Owners: Phil & Kelly Weinberger

Winemaker: Phil Weinberger

Region: West

Established: 1998

Vineyard Acreage: 5 acres

Annual Production: 700 cases

The beautiful property on which Monserrat Vineyards now sits has a very rich and interesting history. The land was first settled in 1842 by James Gallaher. Four years later, James passed away, leaving the property to his wife, Mary Gallaher, and eventually the property landed in the hands of her son, John Gallaher. In 1876, John subdivided part of the 80-acre property as "Gallaher's First Addition to the Town of Montserrat." It is said that John named the new town Montserrat because it reminded him of the mountains surrounding the Monastery of Montserrat in Spain.

John died during the last days of the 19th century, but the beauty of the property flourished. Its gardens were unparalleled in the county and a grand Victorian-style gazebo dominated the scene. In fact, the structure is pictured in the Johnson County Historical Society records. For most of the following century, the property passed from owner to owner, with at least six different families occupying it, and it gradually deteriorated.

Fortunately for wine lovers, the seeds of Montserrat were planted in August 1980, when the property was purchased by the Pearson family. The Pearsons cleared overgrown brush, scrub, and fencing from the property, and planted the first two acres of grapevines on it, though the vineyard eventually grew to three acres. Because of the blueberries also grown on the farm, the Pearsons' property came to be called "Blueberry Hill Farm."

In 1994, owner and winemaker Phil Weinberger purchased the property from the Pearsons. For nearly three years, he continued to operate Blueberry Hill Farm as the Pearsons had: allowing visitors to pick their own fruits for purchase, which included a wide array of berries as well as Catawba, Niagara, Seyval, Steuben, and Vidal grapes. Weinberger and the property soon saw many changes though, beginning in 1996, when Weinberger married his wife in a beautiful ceremony on the property. After the wedding, the Weinbergers made the decision to focus their efforts on grape growing and winemaking, and in 1997, they expanded their vineyard by replacing the berry and other fruit plants with more grapevines. The very next year, Montserrat became a bonded winery.

Montserrat's vineyard has since been expanded again to add both Norton and Traminette grapevines, and the winery is rapidly approaching 1,000 cases of wine produced annually. Clearly, wine lovers are enjoying Montserrat wines. Visitors are invited to come to the winery to taste any of the fantastic wines on its wine list, which include three reds (Chambourcin, Felicita!, and Norton), two whites (Mont Blanc and Tré Belle), two blushes (Damifino and Tramonto), and the seasonal, honey-based Mead. Whether enjoying Montserrat wines on the winery's relaxing outdoor terrace or in its beautiful tasting room, Montserrat offers visitors a wonderful experience in every way.

Montserrat Vineyards

104 Northeast 641
Knob Noster, Missouri 65336
(660) 747-9463
www.montserratvineyards.com

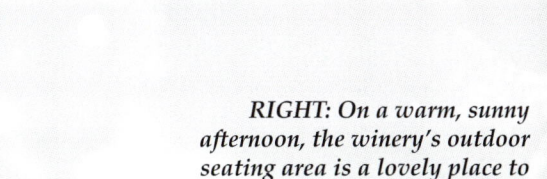

LEFT: The fall is a beautiful time to visit Montserrat.

RIGHT: On a warm, sunny afternoon, the winery's outdoor seating area is a lovely place to enjoy wines.

Grudge myself good wine? As soon grudge my horse corn.

— William Makepeace Thackeray

—158—

New Oak Vineyards

Owners: Tim & Barbara Gasperino

Winemaker: Tim Gasperino

Region: West

Established: 1998

Vineyard Acreage: 11 acres

Annual Production: 4,200 cases

Tucked away in the countryside along the Missouri River, 35 miles east of Kansas City, is a taste of the Old World conveniently located right here in the Midwest. At New Oak Vineyards, owners Tim and Barbara Gasperino have created an atmosphere that lets visitors taste the flavor of northern Italy.

The Gasperinos established New Oak in 1998 with the dream of producing unique, high-quality wines from grapes grown on their fertile land in Lafayette County, near the historic Civil War town of Lexington. Named for the mighty oak trees that help give Missouri wines their unique flavors, New Oak's vineyard grows six grape varietals, including Chambourcin, Chardonel, Norton, Saint Vincent, Seyval, and Vignoles. The vineyard covers 11 acres and borders the winery's beautiful 10-acre lake, the water from which is used to irrigate the grapevines.

New Oak boasts more than just an impressive vineyard and winemaking facility, however, by also featuring a tasting room, banquet hall, gift shop, and outdoor patio. In the winery's tasting room, visitors can sample any wines from New Oak's wine list, which includes six whites (Apple, Chardonel, New Oak Peach, New Oak White, Seyval, and Vignoles), six reds (Chambourcin, Giuseppe, New Oak Red, Norton, Saint Vincent, and Vino Rosa),

—159—

and two blushes (Concord Blush and New Oak Blush). After an afternoon of tasting, visitors are also welcome to purchase in the tasting room each of the New Oak wines that they fell in love with at first taste.

With its bright red table cloths and deep green carpet, New Oak's banquet hall adds a regal touch to any occasion. The hall can accommodate 150 visitors, making it the perfect gathering place for any fun or important event, from business meeting to wedding reception.

The gift shop, located near the tasting room, is a unique and glorious sight. Aside from the giant wine rack running the length of the wall from which visitors can pull a bottle of their favorite New Oak wine, the shop features seating at oak-barrel tables and gifts to entertain any wine lover. Crystal decanters, wineglasses, specialty foods, gift baskets, and more are scattered throughout the shop.

Visitors are also welcome to purchase a bottle of wine to enjoy while relaxing on New Oak's brick patio, where they can soak up the tranquility of the lake and beauty of the lush hillsides surrounding the winery. The patio is also the perfect site for an outdoor wedding ceremony, where the bride and groom can share their vows under the beautiful overhead, wooden trellis. With its serene setting, Old-World elegance, and wonderful wines, New Oak is one of Missouri's finest retreats.

New Oak Vineyards

11644 Flournoy School Road
Wellington, Missouri 64097
(816) 240-2391
www.newoakvineyards.com

BELOW: *The winery offers a great selection of its fine wines for visitors to enjoy.*

"*Wine is a living liquid. When not treated with reasonable respect, it will sicken and die.*

— Julia Child

Odessa Country Winery

Owner: Janice Putnam
Winemaker: Janice Putnam
Region: West

Established: 2007
Vineyard Acreage: 14 acres
Annual Production: 150 cases

Odessa Country Winery is a small-town winery dedicated to producing a specialty line of unique native-American-varietal grape and fruit wines. Its carefully-crafted wines appeal to a large audience with a wide variety of tastes, and the winery maintains a loyal local following of wine lovers who enjoy music, laughter, and great Odessa Country wines.

The winery is owned and managed by Doctor Janice Putnam, who has been involved in vineyard management and wine production since 1996. She gained experience and learned winemaking skills both while employed for several years in various capacities at Bynum Winery and through experimentation in home winemaking. Putnam graciously invites visitors to experience the beauty of Odessa Country and to enjoy all that the winery has to offer. Odessa Country is an artisan winery, producing a line of quality domestic wines made in small batches from local grapes and fruits. While the winery has a large local customer base, it invites and welcomes all visitors. Odessa Country's delicious wines and scenic views encourage relaxation and enjoyment by all.

The winery offers semi-sweet and sweet, country-style wines produced from native-American and European-American hybrid varietals and local fruits. A testament to the quality of its grapes, Odessa Country's red Country Concord and white Diamond were each awarded in statewide competitions in 2006. The winery also offers its Country Cherry Wine, Odessa Puddle Jumping Pear, and Old Fashion Elderberry Wine. All of its wines are reasonably priced and may be purchased and either enjoyed at the winery or taken home for future enjoyment.

Each of Odessa Country's wines may be tasted in the

winery's charming tasting room. Accented with natural wood for a rustic feel, visitors always appreciate the peaceful and calm atmosphere while tasting the delicious wines. Because of Odessa Country's focus on quality rather than quantity, visitors often have the opportunity to unwind privately with a bottle in the tasting room, but always have the opportunity to do so free from the hustle and bustle found at larger wineries.

For those interested in learning about the winemaking process, Odessa Country proudly offers visitors the opportunity to view its winemaking equipment, including the fruit crusher and other interesting pieces. As a more personal touch, Putnam enjoys personally greeting visitors and answering their questions about the winery and the work that goes into each bottle of Odessa Country wine, as well as which of its wines best complement different foods. For wine lovers looking for that personal touch, Odessa Country is clearly not to be missed.

Odessa Country Winery

2466 McNeel Road
Odessa, Missouri 64076
(816) 230-7843
www.odessacountrywinery.com

ABOVE: Odessa Country's tasting room bar is a comfortable place to sample wonderful wines.

RIGHT: The winery's grapes themselves have won numerous awards for their quality.

Drinking wine is just a part of life, like eating food.

— Francis Ford Coppola

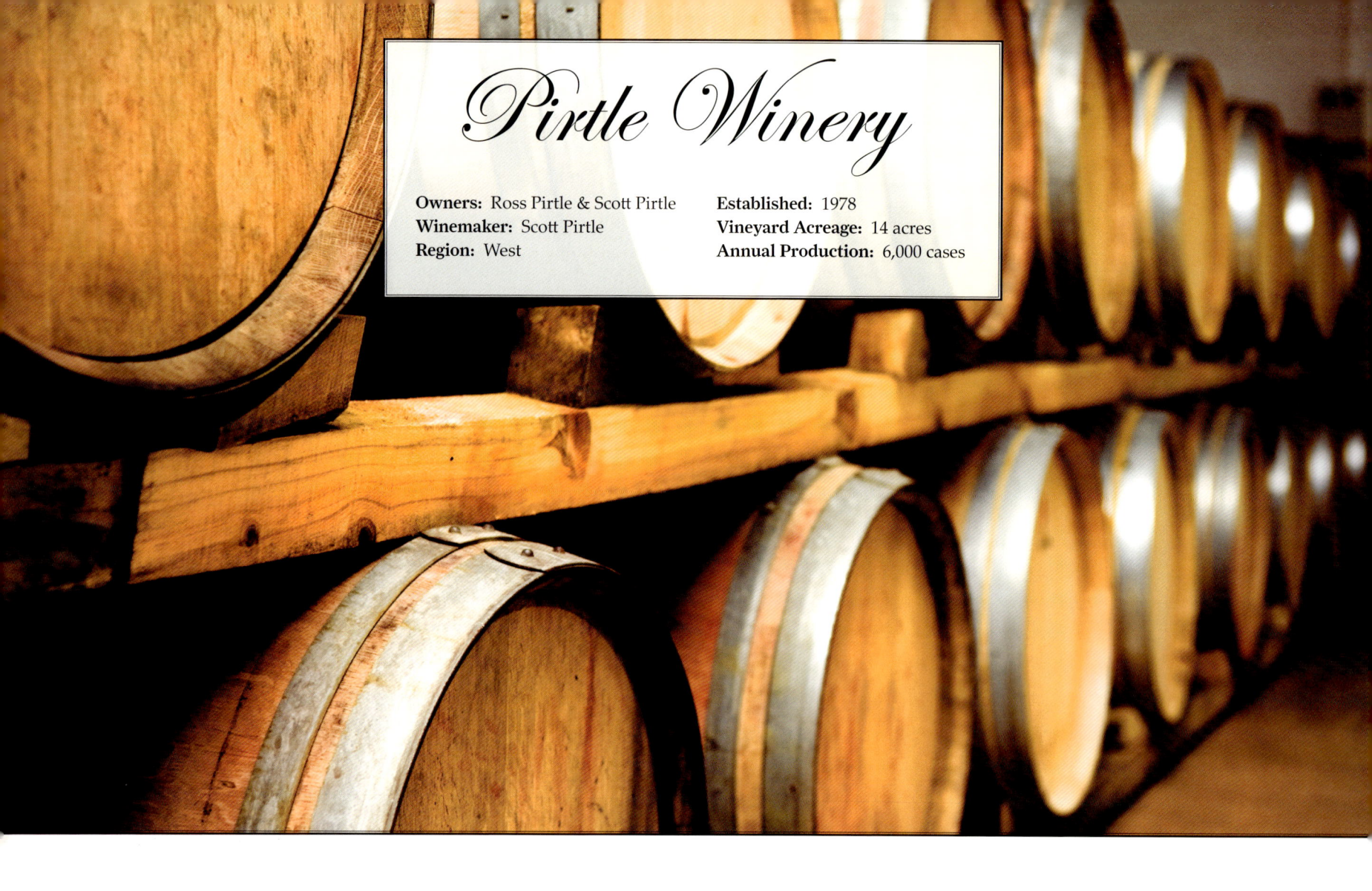

Pirtle Winery

Owners: Ross Pirtle & Scott Pirtle
Winemaker: Scott Pirtle
Region: West
Established: 1978
Vineyard Acreage: 14 acres
Annual Production: 6,000 cases

The characteristic Old-World architecture of the town of Weston enchants visitors and leaves no wonder why the town has a place on the National Register of Historic Places. At the time of its founding, in 1837, it was the most westerly town in the Union. Pirtle Winery, which occupies a quaint building constructed in 1867 as a church by Lutheran-Evangelical immigrants from Germany, maintains the same 19th-century charm as the rest of Weston.

When owners Ross Pirtle and Scott Pirtle founded the winery in 1978, they began a tradition of winemaking in a town with a bit of alcohol already in its blood. Weston Brewing Company, promoted as the "oldest brewery west of the Hudson River," was established in 1842, preceding Anheuser-Busch by 10 years, and sponsored the first Kansas City Royals baseball team. McCormick Distilling Company, also located in Weston, began making premium whiskey in 1856 using water from the natural limestone springs found in the nearby hills of northwest Missouri. It is even rumored that the land which Weston occupies was once purchased for a barrel of whiskey.

It is no surprise that the Pirtles thought that Weston might be an ideal town to support the winery. When visitors walk up the front steps and through the entrance of the red-brick winery, which features beautiful stained-glass windows, they find an enticing tasting room and a lovely gift shop located directly above where Pirtle wines are actually produced.

Pirtle prides itself on its attention to detail throughout the winemaking process, and this attention to detail has not gone unnoticed by critics. The winery's mead wines, which are made from honey and believed to be the preferred drink of the ancient Greeks, are its most-honored specialties. Recently, Pirtle's Blackberry Mead was awarded a gold medal in the Berry Melomel category at the 2008 International Mead Festival in Colorado, adding yet another award to a long list for its meads, every different type of which has been awarded.

In addition to mead wines, Pirtle offers a splendid selection of grape wines, including Chambourcin, Mellow Red, Premium Port, Seyval, and Weston Bend White. The winery also uses fresh, locally-grown fruits to produce its Apple, Blueberry, Cherry, and Effervescent Blueberry wines.

After a long day of wine tasting, touring Pirtle, and taking in all the history and wonder of Weston, visitors can stroll across the road from the winery for fine dining at The Vineyards, a four-star restaurant featuring most of Pirtle's wines on its wine list. No trip to western Missouri is complete without a stop at Pirtle.

Pirtle Winery
502 Spring Street
Weston, Missouri 64098
(816) 640-5728
www.pirtlewinery.com

LEFT: Pirtle takes great pride in its amazing wines.

BELOW: Pirtle carefully tends its vineyards to ensure great grapes for its great wines.

BELOW: Whether with friends, family, or that special someone, the winery provides the perfect atmosphere to enjoy a bottle of wine.

> *Good wine is a necessity of life for me.*
> —Thomas Jefferson

Riverwood Winery

Owners: David Naatz
& Ginah Mortensen

Winemakers: David Naatz
& Ginah Mortensen

Region: West

Established: 2007

Vineyard Acreage: 5 acres

Annual Production: 250 cases

The Missouri River bluffs provide a striking backdrop for Riverwood Winery. Located north of Kansas City, off Highway 45, the winery is surrounded by beauty that changes with each season. In the fall and winter months, bald eagles and flocks of snow geese are constantly seen floating overhead. As the weather warms, the spring and summer months bring bluebirds and other gifts from nature to the area. No matter the season though, visitors can always find a wonderful experience, complete with fine wines, at Riverwood Winery.

At one time, the building that Riverwood now calls home was the site of a schoolhouse, designed in the 1950s by Joseph Radotinsy, who served as the architect for the state of Kansas. Owners and winemakers David Naatz and Ginah Mortensen had other plans for the property, however, when they purchased it in 2005. In addition to renovating the building to meet the needs of the winery, they planted a small vineyard just outside, which is supplemented by a four-acre vineyard a few miles away.

From the grapes grown in these vineyards, as well as some grown in other vineyards, Riverwood produces nine different wines. Among its dry wines are Dry Witty White, which is said to pair perfectly with conversation, and Radiant Red, a bold wine with hints of chocolate. The semi-sweet Ambivalent White balances spicy dishes and barbequed foods, while the winery's sweet wines, such as its Blush of Innocence and Buoyant Blackberry, provide excellent finishing touches to a meal. In addition to its wines, Riverwood also serves imported and locally-made beers and delicious foods, such as free-range, pasture-raised beef.

Visitors enjoy the little extras offered at the winery. Whether it is demonstrations in pairing wines with different foods or wine, cheese, or olive oil tastings, there is always something special and fun happening at Riverwood. The winery's beautiful setting also makes it a popular location for wedding receptions, private parties, and even corporate events.

Located less than three miles from Snow Creek, Riverwood offers skiers a great retreat after a long day on the slopes, and its close proximity to the town of Weston gives visitors the opportunity to visit the town's antique shops and other attractions during a weekend escape to the winery. With so much to offer in such beauty, Riverwood keeps visitors coming back again and again.

Riverwood Winery

22200 Highway 45 North
Rushville, Missouri 64484
(816) 579-9797
www.riverwoodwinery.com

ABOVE: Riverwood's visitors can enjoy views of the beautiful, Missouri countryside.

LEFT: The vineyard is conveniently located for enjoyment by all visitors.

A waltz and a glass of wine can invite an encore.

— Johann Strauss

Stonehaus Farms Vineyard & Winery

Owners: Brett Euritt & Doug Euritt

Winemaker: Doug Euritt

Region: West

Established: 1997

Vineyard Acreage: 6 acres

Annual Production: 1,600 cases

The beautiful country setting of Stonehaus Farms Vineyard & Winery makes it a perfect retreat for visitors looking to escape the rush of downtown Kansas City, which is located only 20 minutes northwest of the winery. With its picturesque fountains, attractive landscaping, and Tuscan theme, Stonehaus Farms virtually whisks its visitors away to the Italian countryside.

Stonehaus Farms got its start in 1982, when Ken and Carol Euritt, the parents of current owners Brett Euritt and Doug Euritt, purchased the farm with plans to build a commercial winery. Over the next two and a half decades, the winery was constructed and several expansions and additions were made to the processing facility, grounds, and vineyard. In early 2007, Ken and Carol passed the reins to their sons, who took over the business with a commitment to increase production levels to accommodate the many requests of retailers wanting to carry Stonehaus Farms' fine wines. Not only have the Euritt brothers increased wine production, but they have also increased the quality of the already-stellar wines and the selection of wines offered.

Stonehaus Farms has gone back to the roots of

ABOVE: To visitors' delight, Stonehaus Farms offers free tastings of its many award-winning wines.

winemaking to create what the Euritts believe are some of the finest Missouri wines available. The winery now produces its dry whites using the old French method of sur lie, which results in a fuller and more-complex taste. With the additions of Cabernet Franc, Topaz, and Vignoles to its wine list, Stonehaus Farms now offers three dry reds, three dry whites, three semi-sweet whites, two fruit wines, and two dessert wines, most of which are produced using the winery's own grapes.

Stonehaus Farms' property is quite impressive. The main building houses both the production facility and the brand-new tasting room, which features fine Tuscan elegance down to the smallest detail. The winery has two additional facilities that provide wonderful venues for any special event. The Garden Room, which can accommodate up to 48 visitors, provides an intimate and private setting for such events as receptions, banquets, parties, rehearsal dinners, and small weddings. The larger Festhall, which opened in 2005, can accommodate up to 250 visitors in its casual elegance.

With its exceptional wines and beautiful grounds and facilities, Stonehaus Farms is a wonderful destination for any wine lover looking to get away for a day. Visitors may be worlds away from the breathtaking vineyards of Italy, but they will certainly feel much closer in the lovely Tuscan charm of Stonehaus Farms.

Stonehaus Farms Vineyard & Winery

24607 Northeast Colbern Road
Lee's Summit, Missouri 64086
(816) 554-8800
www.stonehausfarms.com

LEFT: The new tasting room is the perfect place to enjoy any fine Stonehaus Farms wine.

What though youth gave love and roses, age still leaves us friends and wine.

— Thomas Moore

Terre Beau Vineyards & Winery

Owner: John Tulipana
Winemakers: John Tulipana & Michael Tulipana
Region: West

Established: 2007
Vineyard Acreage: 8 acres
Annual Production: 950 cases

Although Terre Beau Vineyards & Winery has only been open to the public since February 2007, the winery is anything but lacking in history. The building that houses the winery was originally built in 1858 as a place of worship for Presbyterian pioneers exploring westward, making Terre Beau the only Missouri winery located in what was, at one time, a church.

In 2003, John Tulipana planted the first grapevines on the Tulipana family farm, which is located a half mile east of Dover. As soon as the eight acres of vines were producing enough grapes, John and his brother, Michael Tulipana, jumped right into making wines from the grapes. In early 2007, when the Tulipanas became confident in the quality of their wines, they opened Terre Beau to the public.

During the Civil War, the Union Army rounded up Confederate sympathizers from Dover and the surrounding area and held them prisoner in the church until they could be transported to the federal courthouse in Lexington. By 1900, the Presbyterian congregation had diminished, a natural result of Dover's dwindling population, which caused a reduction in Dover's status from a town to a village. However, in 1904, the Catholic Diocese of Kansas City purchased the church and established the Catholic parish of St. John the Baptist.

Eventually, the Tulipanas purchased the church for the purpose of turning it into a winery. Not surprisingly, the building needed renovation in order to accommodate Terre Beau. The Tulipanas were careful during the renovation, though, to ensure that the building maintained its original charm. Today, visitors will find Terre Beau's winemaking facility, tasting room, gift shop, and banquet hall in the historic building. Outside the building, visitors can bask in the warm sunlight as they sip a wonderful glass of Terre Beau wine on the patio or in the picturesque wine garden.

The only difficult part of a visit to Terre Beau is trying to decide which of its great wines to try next. The winery produces Cannonball Red (a sweet red made from Concord grapes), Chambourcin (a semi-dry, medium-body red), Chardonel (a semi-dry, full-body white), Lafayette Red (a semi-sweet red, and Terre Beau's most popular wine), and Norton (a dry, full-body red). Enjoying any of these pleasing wines in such a beautiful and historic setting makes Terre Beau a wonderful choice for any wine lover.

LEFT: Terre Beau's banquet hall is a beautiful venue for a reception or other gathering.

Terre Beau Vineyards & Winery

100 South Lynn
Dover, Missouri 64022
(660) 259-3010
www.terrebeauvineyards.com

LEFT: In Terre Beau's tasting room and gift shop, visitors can sample great wines while picking out the perfect souvenir.

"*That hill over there would be a good place for grapes.*

— Terre Beau owner and winemaker John Tulipana's grandfather, upon first seeing the future site of Terre Beau's vineyard.

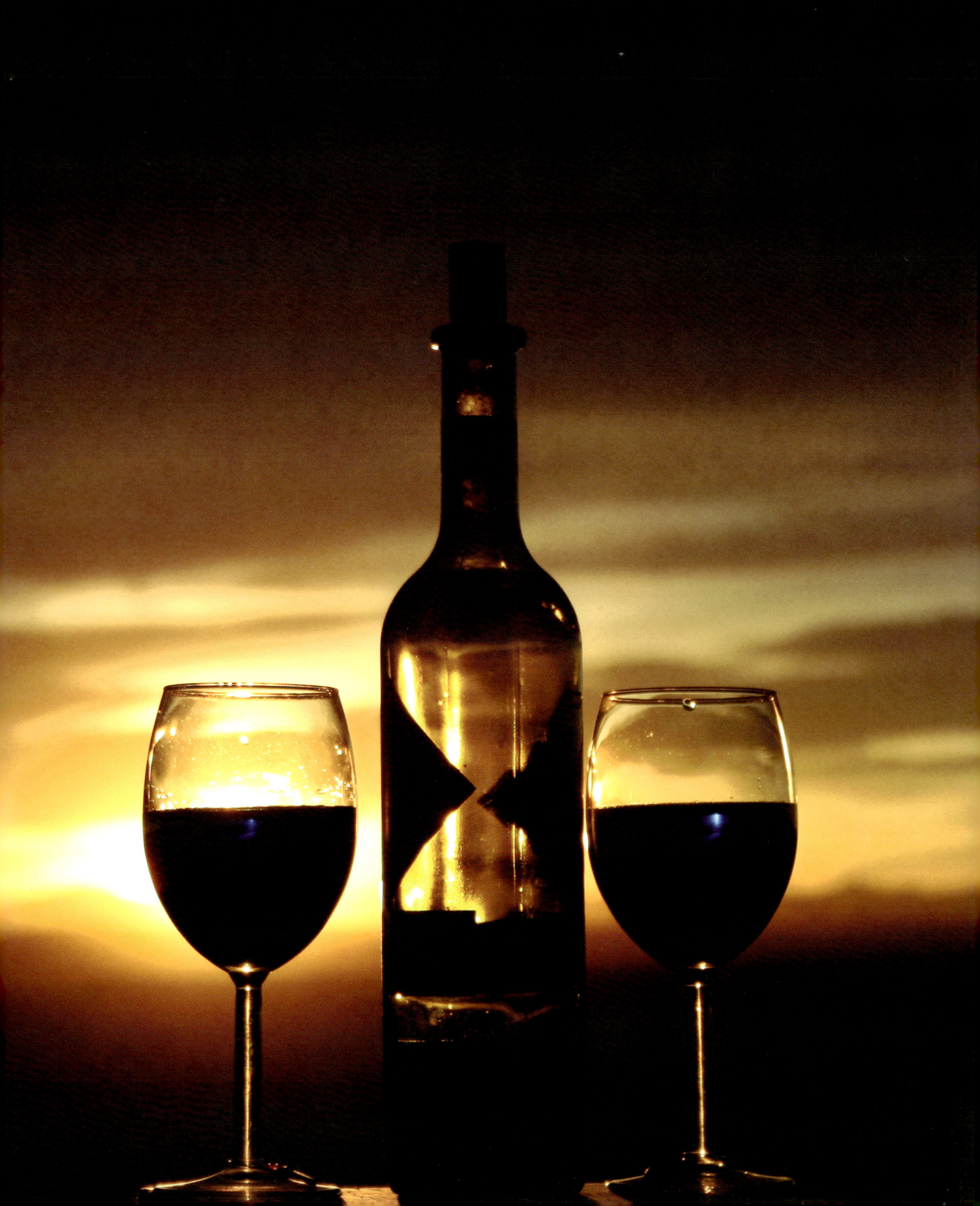

... to wineglass.